This book is from
the kitchen library of

ALSO BY ART GINSBURG, **Mr. Food®**

The **Mr. Food®** Cookbook, **"OOH IT'S SO GOOD!!®"** (1990)

Mr. Food® Cooks Like Mama (1992)

Mr. Food® Cooks Chicken (1993)

Mr. Food® Cooks Pasta (1993)

Mr. Food® Makes Dessert (1993)

Mr. Food® Cooks Real American (1994)

Mr. Food®'s Favorite Cookies (1994)

Mr. Food®'s Quick and Easy Side Dishes (1995)

Mr. Food® Grills It All in a Snap (1995)

Mr. Food®'s Fun Kitchen Tips and Shortcuts
(and Recipes, Too!) (1995)

Mr. Food®'s Old World Cooking Made Easy (1995)

"Help, **Mr. Food®**! Company's Coming!" (1995)

Mr. Food®: Pizza 1-2-3 (1996)

Mr. Food®: Meat Around the Table (1996)

William Morrow and Company, Inc.
New York

It is the policy of William Morrow and Company, Inc., and its imprints and affiliates, recognizing the importance of preserving what has been written, to print the books we publish on acid-free paper, and we exert our best efforts to that end.

Library of Congress Cataloging-in-Publication Data

Ginsburg, Art.

Mr. Food® simply chocolate / Art Ginsburg.—1st ed.

p. cm.

Includes index.

ISBN 0-688-14419-5

1. Cookery (Chocolate) I. Title.

TX767.C5G56 1996 96-7180

641.6'374—dc20 CIP

Printed in the United States of America

2 3 4 5 6 7 8 9 10

BOOK DESIGN BY MICHAEL MENDELSOHN OF MM DESIGN 2000, INC.

Dedicated to

My favorite "children-in-law"—

Carol, Roy, and Tammy

Who also happen to be my favorite chocoholics!

Acknowledgments

I can't believe it! This is my sixteenth book, and I owe a big thank-you to all of my readers and TV viewers who have shared endless recipe ideas and secrets with me over the years. I've tried a load of your chocolate suggestions and, along with my dynamite recipe-testing team of Patty Rosenthal, Janice Bruce, Mike Arnaud, and team captain Joe Peppi, I've come up with a super chocolate recipe collection that's sure to please the most discriminating chocoholics.

Yes, my recipe testers help me work and rework each recipe until we get it just right. Their enthusiasm and creativity, as well as that of the entire **Mr. Food®** team, is never-ending. And since creating a cookbook takes a great deal of input and support from many directions, I want to thank my staff and family for shining through for me once again.

Oh, did I mention that everybody on my team loves chocolate? Sure, they all have their favorite types of chocolate—from smooth milk chocolate to rich, fudgy chocolate to bittersweet chocolate—but they're all confessed chocoholics who had a lot to do with which recipes were included here. Laura Ratcliff, Marilyn Ruderman, Beth Ives, Stacey Dempsey, Steve, Chuck, and Ethel Ginsburg, Tom Palombo, and Roy Fantel . . . thank you.

Al Marchioni and the gang at William Morrow, led by Zachary Schisgal, Richard Aquan, Skip Dye, and Deborah Weiss Geline, always put the icing on the cake. And I love how book designer Michael Mendelsohn and illustrator Philip Scheuer make it all look so appealing. My agent, Bill Adler, and my publicist, Phyllis Heller, always make each book and publicity tour as easy as pie for me.

To top everything off, again I want to thank Howard Rosenthal and Caryl Ginsburg Fantel, who, together, turned my ideas and words into *Simply Chocolate.*

I also want to express my sincerest appreciation to the individuals and companies who have shared their super chocolate products and ideas with me:

Borden

Comstock Michigan Fruit

Dairy Management Inc.

Hershey Foods Corporation

Land O'Lakes, Inc.

Pat Higgins

Pepperidge Farms

SACO Foods, Inc., makers of Real Semisweet Chocolate Chunks

And now, a special thank-you is extended to the Hershey Foods Corporation for providing the miniature chocolate kisses used on the cover of this book. (Boy, was that a fun, yummy photo shoot!)

Contents

Introduction

Chocolate . . . just the mention of that word can quiet an entire party and send shivers up the spines of chocoholics. And I know there are a lot of *those* around!

Actually, most of us probably have a touch of chocoholism. I mean, how could we not get excited when we see and smell luscious chocolate pies, puddings, drinks, cakes, candies, and concoctions. Don't believe me? I dare you to flip through these pages and *not* be tempted!

I start off with my collection of **Heavenly Hodgepodge.** From Fabulous Chocolate Fondue (page 3) and Magic Mocha Mousse (page 8) to Cranberry Chocolate Bread (page 15), these are truly tempting treats that are all special and unique.

Now you must know that serious chocoholics have been known to fantasize about chocolate, and nothing goes better with chocolate than ice cream. That's why I've got some chilly recipes in **Frozen Fantasies** that'll have you guarding your freezer door!

Talk about dreamy . . . In **My Best Brownies and Bars,** there's everything from rich and fudgy squares to bars simply studded with chocolate. They're perfect for that something that can go from freezer to dessert table in no time. You can even rewarm them slightly in the oven or microwave to return that fresh-baked taste.

I think we'd all agree that **Chocolate Takes the Cake.** But all cakes are *not* created equal, especially not these! I've got lots of chocolate cake choices for you. Some are layered, others rolled. Some are light, some rich, and others are nutty. It'll be tough to decide which to make first!

What *won't* be tough is making my pies. You know, if it weren't already popular, that expression "easy as pie" would have started here. In my chapter **Easy as Pie,** there are pies packed with chocolate and cream, and ones like Chocolate Pecan Pie (page 104) that are new twists on old favorites. I'm even sharing my recipe for simple homemade chocolate pie crust . . . and, yes, all can be whipped up in minutes.

We sure have come a long way from the time, in 1930, when Ruth Wakefield made the first of those now-world-famous chocolate chip cookies at her Toll House Inn. We've got so many super cookie choices today. My Chocolate Macadamia Cookies (page 112), Devilish Minty Cookies (page 111), Twisted Chocolate Pretzel Cookies (page 121), and other **Cookie Jar Favorites** are guaranteed to bring out the kid in all of us! Sure, sometimes we like our cookies all by themselves, but when I think of ones like Chocolate Biscotti (page 114), I automatically think about dunking. Why not follow your favorite cookies with the most comforting, homey chocolate drinks you could imagine? Just like I did. Whether you feel like a warming Mochachino (page 134) or a frosty New York Egg Cream (page 135), I'm sure you'll find a drink that fits when you visit **The Chocolate "Bar."**

Did you know that chocolate melts at about 92°F.? Know why that's important? Because at room temperature, it's solid. But when it hits our mouths . . . it melts! So, when you really feel like indulging yourself, try some of my **Melt-in-Your-Mouth Treats.** These are like the candies and fudges that you can buy in gourmet candy shops—except mine are easy and less expensive to make!

Speaking of fancy candies reminds me to tell you that really good chocolate is made all over the world now, with some of the best made right here in the United States. When I talk about chocolate, I'm not referring to that from a particular country, or even a specific brand or type. But if you want to know more about the types of chocolate that are available right on our supermarket shelves, just look at the next few pages. (You'll get some tips on how to best store our great chocolate products, too!)

Finally, I've got **Sinful Sauces, Frostings, and Glazes** for you to mix and match with your cakes, cookies, brownies . . . whatever! And when you add these yummy accents, you'll be topping off your goodies in luscious style.

Okay—enough willpower! You're through reading and can get going on creating your *Simply Chocolate* **"OOH IT'S SO GOOD!!®"**

Chocolate Bits and Bites

Chocolate Choices

For hundreds of years—ever since cocoa beans (the raw product from which chocolate is derived) were used as food *and* money—chocolate has had many admirers. Chocolate has come a long way, and with today's advanced technology, the popularity of chocolate products is never-ending. As I mentioned earlier, chocolate lovers seem to be very clear about the types of chocolate they prefer.

The following chocolate products are readily available right at your supermarket in a variety of forms, which are used in so many different ways. Flavor and texture may vary from brand to brand. Here are the most widely found forms and uses:

Cocoa—An all-purpose unsweetened fine powder that is ground from roasted cocoa beans. It contains almost no cocoa butter.

Unsweetened chocolate—Available in individually wrapped 1-ounce squares, this is often referred to as baking, bitter, or cooking chocolate. It's ideal for brownies, cookies, fudge, cakes, sauces, and more.

Liquid unsweetened chocolate—Packaged in 1-ounce envelopes, this requires no melting, which makes it convenient to use by squeezing it right from the package as needed. One envelope of this can usually be substituted for 1 square of unsweetened chocolate or ¼ cup (dry) cocoa in a recipe.

Semisweet chocolate—Available in pieces (chips and chunks), bars, and squares (like unsweetened chocolate), this is good for eating as is, as well as for baking. Because it melts well, it's used for candies and sauces and is often used for dipping candies and fruits. Semisweet chocolate pieces also hold their shape well in cakes and cookies baked at moderate oven temperatures.

Sweet chocolate—Available in sectioned bars, this is often also called sweet cooking chocolate. It's a combination of unsweetened chocolate, sugar, cocoa butter, and vanilla extract, and it is perfect for eating as is or for giving a rich, chocolate flavor to cakes, pies, sauces, and frostings.

Milk chocolate—Available in a variety of forms, including pieces (chips and chunks), candies, and bars, this is the most popular type used in candy bars. It has added cream, making it lighter in color and milder in taste than sweet and other types of chocolate.

Chocolate-flavored syrup—Available in cans or plastic squeeze bottles, its main ingredient is corn syrup. Other ingredients are cocoa, preservatives, emulsifiers, and flavorings. This product is more widely available on today's supermarket shelves than true chocolate syrups and is most commonly added to milk to make chocolate milk; it's also ready-to-go for drizzling over ice cream, cakes, and other desserts.

Carob—Not "real" chocolate at all, but it has something of a chocolate flavor, so it's often used as a substitute product. While chocolate contains caffeine, carob is made from the locust bean, so it typically contains no caffeine.

White chocolate—The debate continues as to whether or not this is a chocolate product, since it's a combination of milk or cream and sugar blended with cocoa butter and/or various oils. Available as white baking bars, squares, and chips, it's a great addition to cookies and cakes.

Sweetened cocoa powder and instant cocoa mixes—These are dry mixes for making rich chocolate milk and hot chocolate. They are available in bulk as well as individual serving-size packages. Typically consisting of cocoa, flavorings, sugar (although many brands are available in sugar-free blends), and often, powdered milk, most simply require the addition of cold milk or hot water.

Chocolate's "Hot," So Keep It Cool

As with other foods, it's important to store chocolate properly. So here are a few tips for keeping it fresh-looking and fresh-tasting:

- Store chocolate in a cool, dry place (65°F. to 75°F. is ideal).
- If your kitchen is hot, it may be better to refrigerate your chocolate. But first place it in an airtight container so it won't pick up odors and flavors from other foods and from the refrigerator.
- Sometimes chocolate develops a grayish-white film after being refrigerated or stored at too warm or cool a temperature. This doesn't affect the taste, only the appearance of the chocolate. It can be eaten that way, but melting it will return the chocolate to its original color.
- If stored properly, chocolate products such as baking chocolate and cocoa powder will generally stay fresh for up to one year.

First Impressions

This cookbook is packed with quick, easy, tasty recipes that look mighty tempting when served as they are. But since we eat with our eyes, why not give them an extra WOW?! Let me share a few garnishing tips that'll help make their first impressions into lasting impressions (and you won't need any fancy gadgets or long lists of instructions!):

Chocolate curls—No, this isn't a new weight-lifting technique! It's a way to make festive curls of chocolate simply by drawing a vegetable peeler over a room-temperature chocolate bar. Be careful with the curls, because they're very delicate. I think it's easiest to make the curls directly over the item being garnished.

Dusting—It seems like it's always time to dust . . . the tops of our chocolate treats, I mean. It's easy—just place hot chocolate mix, baking cocoa, or confectioners' sugar in a small strainer and gently tap with your finger over a cake or cookies. To get really fancy, place a paper doily on top of a cake and dust with one of the suggested powders; then carefully remove the doily. (The doily acts as a stencil.)

Chocolate cut-outs—Melt 4 ounces semisweet chocolate and 1 ounce unsweetened chocolate in the top of a double boiler over hot water, stirring frequently until melted. Remove from the heat, let cool slightly, and pour onto a rimmed cookie sheet that has been lined with waxed paper; spread to ¼-inch thickness (not necessarily to the edges of the pan), then let cool completely at room temperature. Use a cookie cutter or knife to cut out shapes. These make great garnishes, since you can lay them flat or stand them up alongside or on top of cakes, pies, or even mousses.

Packaged Foods Note

Packaged food sizes may vary by brand. Generally, the sizes indicated in these recipes are average sizes. If you can't find the exact package size listed in the ingredients, whatever package is closest in size will usually do the trick.

Heavenly Hodgepodge

Experience chocolate in so many different ways—as fondue, in pancakes, breads, a fabulous cream puff ring . . . and even in chili!

Fabulous Chocolate Fondue

$4\frac{1}{2}$ cups

You want to serve something different for dessert? Try serving this festive fondue with strawberries and pound cake chunks. Why, you may have to make a double batch to satisfy your chocolate-loving guests!

$1\frac{1}{3}$ cups light corn syrup
$\frac{1}{2}$ pint (1 cup) heavy cream
4 cups (24 ounces) semisweet chocolate chips
1 teaspoon vanilla extract

In a medium-sized saucepan, bring the corn syrup and heavy cream to a boil over medium heat. Remove from the heat and add the chocolate chips and vanilla; stir until the mixture is thick and smooth. Serve in a fondue pot or in a heatproof bowl on an electric warming tray and stir occasionally. **Always use caution when using a warming tray.**

NOTE: Chocolate fondue dippers can include chunks of pound cake and cookies, or even marshmallows and fruit slices. Whole fresh strawberries and chunks of pineapple and bananas are especially good partners. Be creative—try different combinations to come up with your own favorites!

Chocolate Crème Caramel

8 to 10 servings

The cocoa powder puts this traditional favorite into a class by itself—a class that's sure to win high marks from you!

¾ cup sugar, divided
4 eggs
1 teaspoon vanilla extract
¼ cup sweetened cocoa powder or hot chocolate mix
2 cups milk

Preheat the oven to 350°F. In a small nonstick skillet, stir ½ cup sugar over medium heat for about 6 minutes, until completely melted and caramel-colored. Immediately pour the melted sugar into a 9-inch glass pie plate, completely coating the bottom of the plate. **Be careful when working with the caramelized sugar; it is very hot.** In a medium-sized bowl, beat the eggs and vanilla well with an electric beater on medium speed. In a medium-sized bowl, combine the cocoa and the remaining sugar; mix well with a spoon. Stir in the milk, then beat into the egg mixture. Pour over the caramelized sugar and place the pie plate in a roasting pan. Pour water into the roasting pan to go about halfway up the sides of the pie plate, being careful not to pour water into the pie plate. Bake for 45 to 50 minutes, or until a knife inserted in the center of the crème caramel comes out clean. Carefully remove the pie plate from the water and let cool for 20 minutes, then cover and chill for at least 1 hour before serving. Just before serving, run a table knife around the inside edge of the pie plate to loosen the custard from the plate. Carefully invert the crème caramel onto a 10- to 12-inch rimmed serving plate, so that the caramel sauce doesn't run off the plate (see Note). Serve each wedge with some of the caramel sauce.

NOTE: The best way to remove the crème caramel from the pie plate is to place the serving plate upside down over the top of the pie plate and, holding the two together tightly, turn them over quickly. Then slowly remove the pie plate.

Almost-Belgian Chocolate Mousse

6 to 8 servings

This recipe from my Old World cookbook has received so many raves that I just had to give you another opportunity to try it. One taste and you'll know why it's so popular!

1 cup (6 ounces) semisweet chocolate chips
1 pint (2 cups) heavy cream
$\frac{1}{8}$ teaspoon instant coffee granules
1 teaspoon warm water

In a small saucepan, melt the chocolate over low heat until smooth, stirring constantly. Set aside until slightly cooled. Place the heavy cream in a large bowl and beat with an electric beater until soft peaks form. Gently fold in the chocolate. In a cup, dissolve the instant coffee in the water, then gently fold into the chocolate mixture. Cover and refrigerate until ready to serve.

NOTE: For an extra-special way to serve this, spoon it into individual serving cups and top with some additional whipped cream. It's also nice to add a European touch by grating a bit of a chocolate bar over the top of each.

White Chocolate Mousse

6 to 8 servings

Mention white chocolate and people think they're in for something very upscale and fancy. White chocolate mousse does the same thing. Why? Because it tastes like it's fit for royalty!

1 package (6 ounces) white baking bars
1 pint (2 cups) heavy cream, divided
1/3 cup confectioners' sugar
1 teaspoon vanilla extract

In a medium-sized saucepan, combine the baking bars and 1/2 cup heavy cream over low heat, stirring constantly until the bars are melted and the mixture is smooth. Remove from the heat and let cool completely. In a medium-sized bowl, with an electric beater on medium speed, beat the confectioners' sugar, vanilla, and the remaining cream until stiff peaks form. Gently fold the white chocolate mixture into the whipped cream until blended; do not stir. Cover and chill for at least 2 hours before serving.

NOTE: For a truly royal dessert, serve this mousse in Special Occasion Chocolate Cups (page 158) on a pool of Raspberry Sauce (page 163).

Magic Mocha Mousse

6 to 8 servings

Not only is this a flavor-packed teaming of chocolate and coffee, but when you taste it you'll discover the magic.

3 squares (1 ounce each) semisweet chocolate
4 ounces cream cheese, softened
1 tablespoon instant coffee granules
2 tablespoons hot water
1 teaspoon vanilla extract
1 jar (7 ounces) marshmallow creme
1 container (8 ounces) frozen whipped topping, thawed

In a large microwave-safe bowl, heat the chocolate in the microwave on high power for 1½ to 2 minutes; stir the chocolate until completely melted and smooth. Add the cream cheese and mix with an electric beater on medium speed until well blended. In a cup, dissolve the coffee in the hot water, and add to the cream cheese mixture. Add the vanilla and beat until well combined. Blend in the marshmallow creme, then fold in the whipped topping. Cover and refrigerate for at least 1 hour before serving.

NOTE: Serve this alone or with crisp cookies. And it can be made and served just as easily in individual dessert dishes. Top each with an extra dollop of whipped topping!

Chocolate Orange Whip

8 servings

Not all chocolate desserts are heavy and rich, and this one proves it. It's light and refreshing, and its hint of orange makes it the perfect dessert even when nobody has much room left!

$\frac{1}{3}$ cup sugar
$\frac{1}{4}$ cup unsweetened cocoa
1 envelope (0.25 ounce) unflavored gelatin
2 cups skim milk
1 teaspoon vanilla extract
$\frac{1}{4}$ teaspoon orange extract
$1\frac{1}{2}$ cups frozen whipped topping, thawed

In a medium-sized saucepan, combine the sugar, cocoa, and gelatin. Stir in the milk and let stand for 2 minutes to soften the gelatin. Cook over medium heat for about 5 minutes, stirring constantly until the gelatin is completely dissolved. Pour the mixture into a medium-sized bowl, then stir in the vanilla and orange extracts. Chill for about 30 minutes, stirring every few minutes, until the mixture mounds when dropped from a spoon. Do not allow the mixture to gel. Add the whipped topping to the chocolate mixture and beat with a wire whisk until well blended. Refrigerate for about 10 minutes, until slightly thickened. Spoon into 8 individual serving dishes, cover, and refrigerate for 3 to 4 hours, until firm.

NOTE: Garnish with additional whipped topping and orange wedges, if desired.

Homemade Chocolate Pudding

4 to 6 servings

Know what? There was homemade pudding before there was pudding in boxes and flip-top cans. And if you want to get back to homemade goodness, try this version that's quick, quick, quick!

2/3 cup sugar
1/4 cup unsweetened cocoa
3 tablespoons cornstarch
1/4 teaspoon salt
2 1/4 cups cold milk
1 teaspoon vanilla extract

In a medium-sized saucepan, combine the sugar, cocoa, cornstarch, and salt. Gradually stir in the milk. Bring to a boil over medium heat, stirring constantly. Remove from the heat and stir in the vanilla. Spoon into 4 to 6 individual serving dishes or 1 large bowl and refrigerate for 2 to 3 hours, or until firm.

NOTE: For a down-home taste, I like to eat this pudding warm, topped with a little ice-cold milk. But for a really elegant look, it's easy to top it with fresh Whipped Cream (page 176) and chocolate curls. To make chocolate curls: Use a vegetable peeler to "peel" a thick 5- to 7-ounce candy bar over the whipped cream.

Family-Sized Death by Chocolate

10 to 12 servings

Yup, Death by Chocolate is back—and better than ever! You don't believe me? Just try it and see!

1 box (21 to 23 ounces) brownie mix, prepared according to the package directions and cooled
1/4 cup coffee liqueur
1 box (4-serving size) instant chocolate pudding and pie filling
1 1/2 cups cold milk
1 container (8 ounces) frozen whipped topping, thawed, divided
4 chocolate-covered toffee candy bars (1.4 ounces each), broken into small pieces

Use a fork to prick holes in the top of the cooled brownies. Pour the liqueur over the top; set aside. In a medium-sized bowl, combine the chocolate pudding mix and milk and stir with a wire whisk until thickened. Fold in half of the whipped topping and set aside. Break up the brownies into small pieces and place half in the bottom of a large glass serving bowl. Cover with the pudding mixture, then half the candy. Place the remaining brownies on top, then cover with the remaining plain whipped topping and sprinkle the remaining candy over the top. Chill for at least 2 hours before serving.

NOTE: Instead of coffee liqueur, you can substitute a mixture of 1 teaspoon sugar and 1/4 cup leftover black coffee, or you could even leave out the coffee flavoring entirely, if you'd prefer.

Chocolate Chip Pancakes

12 to 14 pancakes

Who says chocolate can only be eaten at the end of a meal? I think it's a great way to start off the day!

2 cups biscuit baking mix
1 cup milk
2 eggs
2 teaspoons light brown sugar
2 teaspoons vanilla extract
1 cup (6 ounces) semisweet chocolate chips

In a large bowl, combine all the ingredients except the chocolate chips; mix well with a spoon, then stir in the chocolate chips. Preheat a greased griddle or skillet over medium-high heat. Using 1/4 cup batter for each pancake, pour the batter onto the griddle or skillet. Turn the pancakes after 2 to 3 minutes, when the tops bubble, then cook for an additional 1 to 2 minutes, until golden.

NOTE: For an extra-special treat, top these with Chocolate Maple Syrup (page 167).

Sour Cream–Chocolate Bread

1 loaf

Boy, if you want to have a really special treat this Sunday morning, toast a few slices of this to enjoy along with your hot coffee and Sunday paper. Maybe it's what heaven is like!

½ cup (1 stick) butter, softened
1 cup sugar
2 eggs
1 cup sour cream
1¾ cups all-purpose flour
½ cup unsweetened cocoa
½ teaspoon baking powder
½ teaspoon baking soda

Preheat the oven to 350°F. In a large bowl, cream the butter and sugar with an electric beater on medium speed. Add the eggs and beat until fluffy. Continue beating and add the sour cream. Add the remaining ingredients; mix until well blended. Pour into a 9" × 5" loaf pan that has been coated with nonstick baking spray. Bake for 50 to 55 minutes, or until a wooden toothpick inserted in the center comes out clean. Cool for 15 minutes, then remove from the pan to cool completely on a wire rack.

NOTE: This is great plain, but you might want to try it with a little bit of cream cheese spread on top of each slice.

Double Chocolate Muffins

12 muffins

With these you're in for a super double hit of chocolate! And you know what? I bet you're gonna love it!

1½ cups all-purpose flour
½ cup unsweetened cocoa
⅓ cup sugar
1 tablespoon baking powder
¼ teaspoon salt
2 eggs, beaten
¾ cup milk
½ cup (1 stick) butter, melted
1 cup (6 ounces) semisweet chocolate chips

Preheat the oven to 400°F. In a large bowl, combine the flour, cocoa, sugar, baking powder, and salt; mix well. Add the eggs, milk, and butter; mix well with a spoon. Add the chocolate chips and mix just until combined. Coat a 12-cup muffin tin with nonstick baking spray and fill each cup three-quarters full with batter. Bake for 15 to 20 minutes, or until a wooden toothpick inserted in the center comes out clean. Remove the muffins from the pan and cool on a wire rack.

NOTE: Dust the muffins with a bit of confectioners' sugar for a fancier-looking confection.

Cranberry Chocolate Bread

2 loaves

Watch out! This bread could cause a real frenzy because nobody will be expecting that delicious combination of chocolate and cranberries. They're gonna come running to your door, begging for more! (Good luck!)

2½ cups all-purpose flour
1½ cups sugar
1 tablespoon baking powder
½ cup vegetable shortening
3 eggs
1 cup cranberry juice cocktail
¼ cup chocolate-flavored syrup
1 cup dried cranberries
½ cup (3 ounces) semisweet chocolate chips
½ cup chopped walnuts

Preheat the oven to 350°F. In a large bowl, combine the flour, sugar, and baking powder. With an electric beater, beat in the shortening until smooth. Stir in the eggs, cranberry juice, and chocolate syrup until thoroughly combined. Fold in the cranberries, chocolate chips, and walnuts. Pour the batter into two 8" × 4" loaf pans that have been coated with nonstick baking spray. Bake for 50 to 55 minutes, or until a wooden toothpick inserted in the center comes out clean. Cool for 5 minutes before removing from the pan, then cool completely on a wire rack.

NOTE: By making two loaves, you get an extra chance to enjoy these great flavors. It sure is great to have one on hand in the freezer.

Day-Off Chocolate Croissants

12 croissants

Oh, the smell! Oh, the taste! These are what I look forward to on those rare, lazy holiday mornings when we're not rushed and crazy. I bet these will be the perfect start to a relaxing, wonderful day for you, too. Go on, give them a try!

1 cup (6 ounces) semisweet chocolate chips, divided
Twelve 1-ounce croissants, sliced in half horizontally, then thawed if frozen
¼ cup slivered almonds

In a small microwave-safe bowl, heat ¾ cup chocolate chips in the microwave on high power for about 1 minute. Stir to completely melt the chips; if necessary, heat for additional 10-second intervals until completely melted. Spread an equal amount of the melted chocolate on the cut side of the bottom half of each croissant. Replace the top halves of the croissants. Place the remaining chocolate chips in a heavy-duty resealable plastic storage bag and microwave on high power for 30 seconds; knead the chocolate in the bag until the chips have completely melted. Carefully snip a small hole in the corner of the plastic bag and squeeze the chocolate through the hole, drizzling it over the top of the croissants. Top the croissants with the slivered almonds. Allow the croissants to stand for about 30 minutes, until the chocolate cools and hardens slightly. Serve, or cover until ready to use.

NOTE: Fresh or frozen croissants will work here. But, depending on the size of the croissants, you may have to adjust the quantity of chocolate used. If you make these in advance, maybe you'll want to warm them slightly in the microwave just before serving.

Chocolate Bundles

4 servings

I'm sure you've heard the expression "a bundle of joy." The next time you hear it, it could be referring to these handy little bundles containing bursts of chocolate!

1 sheet (from a 17.25-ounce box) frozen puff pastry dough
1 cup (6 ounces) semisweet chocolate chips
¼ cup chopped walnuts
Confectioners' sugar for sprinkling

Thaw the puff pastry for 30 minutes. Preheat the oven to 425°F. On a lightly floured surface, roll the pastry out to a 12-inch square; cut the square into four 6-inch squares. Place ¼ cup chocolate chips and 1 tablespoon chopped walnuts in the center of each square. Bring the pastry corners together and twist the dough, closing tightly; fan out the corners (see illustration). Place on an ungreased baking sheet and bake for 10 to 15 minutes, or until golden brown. Let stand for 10 minutes, then sprinkle with confectioners' sugar and serve.

NOTE: For best results, these need to be baked just before serving.

Chocolate Roll-ups

16 pastries

When you're not sure what you're hungering for, give these a try. They're a super way to start or end your day—from breakfast to a late-night snack (and, of course, for snack times in between, too).

½ cup (3 ounces) semisweet chocolate chips
1 tablespoon vegetable shortening
1 teaspoon almond extract
1 container (8 ounces) refrigerated crescent dinner rolls (8 rolls)
2 tablespoons sliced almonds
Confectioners' sugar for sprinkling

Preheat the oven to 350°F. In a small saucepan, combine the chocolate chips and shortening over low heat. Heat until the chocolate is melted and the mixture is smooth, stirring constantly. Remove from the heat and stir in the almond extract. Unroll the dinner roll dough and separate it into 8 triangles. Spread the chocolate sauce evenly over each triangle, then sprinkle with the sliced almonds. Cut each triangle in half and roll up, starting at the wide end. Bake on an ungreased cookie sheet for 12 to 15 minutes, or until golden. Sprinkle with confectioners' sugar before serving.

NOTE: Serve these warm or at room temperature. I can't decide which way I like better!

Cream Puff Ring

12 servings

Here's my easy version of what the French call *Gâteau St.-Honoré.* Make this fancy dessert if you want to hear lots of "ooh"s and "aah"s.

1 cup water
½ cup (1 stick) butter, cut into quarters
¼ teaspoon salt
1 cup all-purpose flour
4 eggs, at room temperature
1 package (4-serving size) instant chocolate pudding and pie filling
1 cup cold milk
1 cup frozen whipped topping, thawed
Chocolate Glaze (page 174)

Preheat the oven to 400°F. In a medium-sized saucepan, bring the water, butter, and salt to a boil over medium-high heat. Add the flour all at once and stir quickly with a wooden spoon until the mixture forms a ball; remove from the heat. Add 1 egg to the mixture and beat with the wooden spoon to blend. Add the remaining eggs one at a time, beating well after each addition. When the dough is smooth, spoon out ¼ cup at a time, placing the dough around the outside edge of an ungreased 10-inch pizza pan to form a ring. Each mound of dough should press against the one next to it so that they are all connected. Bake for 40 to 45 minutes, or until golden brown and puffy. Cool on the pizza pan on a wire rack. When the ring is cooled, with a sharp knife, slice all the way around the ring, halfway between the top and bottom and about three quarters of the way through, leaving the inside of the ring intact. In a medium-sized bowl, combine the chocolate pudding mix and milk; mix well. Add the whipped topping and mix until thoroughly combined. Carefully lift the outside edges of the ring, and spoon the chocolate mixture into the ring until it is completely filled. Prepare the Chocolate Glaze and drizzle it over the Cream Puff Ring. Chill for at least 1 hour before serving.

NOTE: You can also make these as individual cream puffs. Just spoon the mounds of dough onto a cookie sheet so that the edges are not touching. When they've finished baking and completely cooled, cut each puff in half horizontally and proceed as above.

Cold Fudge Cake

12 to 15 servings

Here's a family favorite that should be kept under lock and key. I'm afraid that this one will have you and your gang raiding the fridge at night until it's gone!

3/4 cup (1 1/2 sticks) butter
1 1/2 cups all-purpose flour
1 cup chopped walnuts, divided
2 packages (4 servings each) instant chocolate pudding and pie filling
3 cups milk
12 ounces cream cheese, softened
1 cup confectioners' sugar
2 containers (8 ounces each) frozen whipped topping, thawed

Preheat the oven to 350°F. In a medium-sized saucepan, melt the butter over medium-low heat. Remove from the heat and mix in the flour and 3/4 cup nuts. Press the mixture into a 9" × 13" glass baking dish. Bake for 10 to 12 minutes, until the crust is firm, then remove from the oven and let cool. In a medium-sized bowl, combine the chocolate pudding mix and milk and whisk until thickened; set aside. In another medium-sized bowl, combine the cream cheese, confectioners' sugar, and 1 container of whipped topping; mix well. Using a wet table knife, spread the cream cheese mixture over the top of the cooled crust. Spoon the chocolate pudding mixture over the top of the cream cheese mixture, then top with the remaining whipped topping. Sprinkle the remaining walnuts over the top. Cover and refrigerate for at least 6 hours, or overnight. Store any leftovers in the refrigerator.

Chocolate–Peanut Butter Brownie Bowl

10 to 12 servings

This one has layer after layer of two of my favorite tastes. Yours too, I'll bet. Well, no matter how much you like it, be sure to start with a small portion, 'cause it's *soooo* rich.

1 box (21 to 23 ounces) brownie mix, prepared according to the package directions and cooled
1 box (4-serving size) instant chocolate pudding and pie filling, prepared according to the package directions
1 bag (9 ounces) miniature peanut butter cups, chopped
1 container (8 ounces) frozen whipped topping, thawed
1/3 cup creamy peanut butter
1/4 cup unsalted peanuts

Break the cooled brownies into chunks and layer half of them in the bottom of a large glass serving bowl. Cover with half of the prepared pudding, then sprinkle with half of the chopped peanut butter cups. Repeat the layers with the remaining brownies, pudding, and chopped peanut butter cups. In a small bowl, combine the whipped topping with the peanut butter and mix until smooth. Spread the topping mixture over the top and sprinkle with the peanuts. Cover and chill for at least 2 hours before serving. Be sure to refrigerate any leftovers.

NOTE: You can also make these in individual glass serving dishes or parfait glasses so that everybody can see and enjoy their own layers and layers of this peanut buttery treat. And I recommend making the brownies more chewy than cakey; those directions should be right on the package.

Chocolate Play "Clay"

1½ pounds

Wow! I bet this is a new one for you! Just give it a try, and I can promise that your kids and grandkids will love you for it!

1 can (16 ounces) ready-to-spread chocolate frosting
1 cup creamy peanut butter
1½ cups confectioners' sugar

In a large bowl, combine all the ingredients; mix well. It's ready to play with and make into all sorts of fun shapes. Store in an airtight container in the refrigerator.

NOTE: If the kids plan to taste this, they should do so *before* they start playing with it. It should keep for a few weeks if stored as directed.

Cincinnati Chili

4 to 6 servings

Chili . . . in a chocolate book?! Nobody said that this was strictly a dessert book, and chocolate *is* used in foods other than desserts. So here it is—just one more unusual recipe that is "simply chocolate."

1 pound lean ground beef
1 small onion, chopped
1 tablespoon unsweetened cocoa
2 teaspoons chili powder
½ teaspoon cayenne pepper
¼ teaspoon ground allspice
¼ teaspoon ground cinnamon
1 can (28 ounces) crushed tomatoes
1 can (6 ounces) tomato paste
½ cup water
1 tablespoon sugar
½ teaspoon salt

In a large saucepan or soup pot, brown the beef with the onions over medium heat for 6 to 8 minutes, or until no pink remains in the meat. Drain off any excess liquid, then return the saucepan to the stove and add the remaining ingredients; mix well. Bring to a boil, then reduce the heat to low and simmer for 30 minutes, stirring occasionally.

NOTE: This is like the mole flavoring popular in authentic Mexican cooking.

Frozen Fantasies

Dreamy ice cream cakes and novelties, frozen pies, sherbet, and other frozen desserts, teamed with everything from almonds to flavorful raspberries and more!

Secret Peanut Butter Pie

10 to 12 servings

After you make this, your gang's gonna wonder why you've been keeping the recipe a secret from them. Don't worry—I can keep a secret, too!

1⅔ cups (10 ounces) peanut butter chips
½ cup milk
1 can (14 ounces) sweetened condensed milk, divided
2 packages (8 ounces each) cream cheese, softened
1 tablespoon vanilla extract
16 miniature peanut butter cups, coarsely chopped
1 cup frozen whipped topping, thawed
One 9-inch prepared chocolate pie crust

In a medium-sized saucepan, combine the peanut butter chips, milk, and ⅓ cup sweetened condensed milk over low heat. Cook until the mixture is thick and smooth, stirring constantly. Remove the saucepan from the heat and allow the mixture to cool to room temperature. In a large bowl, with an electric beater on medium speed, beat the cream cheese until light and fluffy. Gradually beat in the remaining sweetened condensed milk and the vanilla. With a spoon, stir in the chopped peanut butter cups. Add the whipped topping to the cooled milk mixture and blend completely with a spoon. Gently pour the milk mixture and the cream cheese mixture alternately into the pie crust, ending with the cream cheese mixture. Swirl with a knife to get a marbled effect. Cover and freeze until firm. Let stand at room temperature for 10 minutes before serving.

Chocolate Almond Frozen Bananas

6 to 8 servings

I tried to copy those frozen bananas that we all remember from our old-time country fairs and festivals. Now, if only I had a merry-go-round. . . .

6 to 8 bamboo skewers
3 to 4 large ripe (but firm) bananas
2 cups (12 ounces) semisweet chocolate chips
¼ cup vegetable shortening
1 teaspoon almond extract
¾ cup chopped almonds

Line a rimmed cookie sheet with waxed paper. Cut the bananas in half crosswise and place a skewer lengthwise through the center (beginning at the cut end) of each half. Place on the cookie sheet and freeze for 3 to 4 hours, or overnight. After the bananas have frozen, place the chocolate chips and shortening in a medium-sized microwave-safe bowl. Microwave on high for 1 to 2 minutes, just until the chips are melted. Remove from the microwave and mix until smooth. Add the almond extract and almonds; mix well. Hold each banana by the stick over the bowl of chocolate and spoon the chocolate mixture over the banana, evenly coating it; work fast because the chocolate hardens quickly. Allow the excess to drip off. Lay the coated bananas on the waxed paper–lined cookie sheet and freeze for 45 minutes to 1 hour. Store in resealable plastic storage bags.

NOTE: If you'd prefer to melt the chocolate on the stove top, just place the chocolate and shortening in a medium-sized saucepan and melt over low heat, stirring frequently. Do not allow the mixture to burn. If wrapped tightly, these bananas will last for up to 2 months in the freezer.

Chocolate Cream Freeze

6 to 8 servings

Don't let the sound of the doorbell after dinner scare you anymore—'cause now you've got the answer for drop-in company that comes expecting dessert!

1½ cups crushed chocolate wafer cookies (about 35 wafers)
¼ cup (½ stick) butter, melted
1 pint (2 cups) heavy cream
3 tablespoons sugar
1 cup (6 ounces) semisweet chocolate chips
½ cup finely chopped almonds

In a medium-sized bowl, combine the crushed wafers and butter; mix well. Press the wafer mixture firmly into the bottom and up the sides of a 9-inch pie plate that has been coated with nonstick baking spray; set aside. In a freezer-safe medium-sized bowl, beat the cream with an electric beater until foamy; add the sugar and continue beating until stiff peaks form. Cover and place the cream in the freezer for 2 to 3 hours, or until icy but not completely frozen. In a medium-sized saucepan, melt the chocolate chips over low heat, stirring constantly, and stir in the almonds. While the chocolate mixture is still hot, slowly stir into the icy whipped cream; small chunks of chocolate and almonds will form when the hot and cold mixtures combine. Spoon into the pie crust. Cover with aluminum foil and freeze for 3 to 4 hours, or until ready to serve.

NOTE: Start off by cutting small wedges, because it's so rich. You can always serve seconds.

Chocolate Raspberry Roll

12 to 15 servings

Raspberries and chocolate! Sounds like a combination you'd find at a fancy French restaurant, huh? But you can wow everybody at home with this delicious treat.

1 container (12 ounces) frozen whipped topping, thawed, divided
½ cup raspberry preserves
1 package (9 ounces) chocolate wafer cookies (about 40 wafers)
½ pint fresh raspberries

In a small bowl, combine half the whipped topping and the raspberry preserves; mix well. Spread 1 heaping teaspoon of the mixture on one side of each of 7 wafers, stacking the wafers on top of each other. Place a plain wafer on top, as shown in illustration 1 on the next page. Repeat, using the remaining wafers and whipped topping mixture, making 5 stacks. Carefully turn each stack on its side and place them side by side on a platter. Frost with the remaining plain whipped topping, as shown in illustration 2 on the next page. Freeze for 3 to 4 hours, or overnight. If freezing overnight, make sure to cover well after the whipped topping has set. When ready to serve, cut into slices, as shown in illustration 3 on the next page, then top with the fresh raspberries.

NOTE: This may sound complicated, but it's surprisingly easy. Just follow the directions and refer to the illustrations so you can be on your way to making a special-occasion dessert in no time.

STACK'EM
1
FROST'EM
2
SLICE'EM
3

Hot Fudge Sundae Sandwiches

6 sandwiches

Here's a perfect make-ahead dessert for those times when you're on the go. Fancy it up a bit, and it'll look like you fussed for hours.

One 12- to 16-ounce fresh or frozen pound cake, cut into 12 slices
1 jar (11.75 ounces) hot fudge sauce, warmed
1 quart chocolate ice cream
6 maraschino cherries (optional)

Place the cake slices on a large rimmed cookie sheet. Spread 2 teaspoons of the hot fudge sauce on each slice. Run warm water around the outside of the ice cream container and slide the ice cream out onto its side on a cutting board. Slice into 6 even rounds, each about 1 inch thick. Place a slice of ice cream on each of 6 of the fudge-covered cake slices. Place the other 6 slices of cake over the ice cream, fudge side down. Wrap the sandwiches individually in plastic wrap and freeze for at least 2 hours before serving. To serve, unwrap the sandwiches and place them on a serving plate; rewarm the remaining fudge sauce and drizzle it over the top of each. Top with the cherries, if desired.

Chocolate Chip Ice Cream Sandwiches

12 sandwiches

These could really be called Triple-Chip Ice Cream Sandwiches since there are yummy chocolate chips everywhere—in the cookie dough, in the ice cream, and even around the edges!

1 package (18 ounces) refrigerated chocolate chip cookie dough
1 quart chocolate chip ice cream
1 cup (6 ounces) miniature semisweet chocolate chips

Freeze the dough for several hours to make slicing easier. Preheat the oven to 350°F. Using a sharp knife dipped in hot water, cut the cookie dough into 24 slices, and bake according to the package directions. Remove from the oven and let cool for about 5 minutes before removing from the cookie sheet. Place 1 small scoop of ice cream on an upside-down cookie, then top with a right-side-up cookie. Squeeze the 2 cookies together until the ice cream is pushed to the edges. Place the chocolate chips on a plate and roll the edges of the sandwich over the chips until the chips stick to the ice cream. Lightly press the chips into the ice cream and place the sandwich on a cookie sheet. Place in the freezer. Continue with the remaining cookies, ice cream, and chips. When the sandwiches are frozen, individually wrap them in plastic wrap and keep frozen until ready to serve.

NOTE: If you'd like, you can substitute ½ cup of your favorite chopped nuts for ½ cup of the chocolate chips.

Banana Split Cream Puffs

12 servings

There should be enough here to feed a small party, but don't say I didn't warn you! After they taste these, they won't want to "split"!

1 cup water
½ cup (1 stick) butter, cut into quarters
¼ teaspoon salt
1 cup all-purpose flour
4 eggs, at room temperature
2 large bananas, peeled and sliced into 18 slices each
½ gallon vanilla ice cream
¼ cup strawberry preserves
¾ cup hot fudge sauce, warmed

Preheat the oven to 400°F. In a medium-sized saucepan, bring the water, butter, and salt to a boil over high heat. Add the flour all at once and stir quickly with a wooden spoon until the mixture forms a ball. Remove from the heat. Add 1 egg to the mixture and beat hard with the wooden spoon to blend. Add the remaining eggs one at a time, beating well after each addition. Each egg must be completely blended before the next egg is added. As you beat the mixture, it will change from looking almost curdled to smooth. When it becomes smooth, spoon out ¼ cup of the mixture for each of 12 pastry puffs, spacing the puffs evenly on a large ungreased cookie sheet. Bake for 30 to 35 minutes, until golden and puffed. Cool on a wire rack. Cut each pastry puff horizontally in half and layer 3 banana slices in the bottom of each. Place a large scoop of ice cream into each puff and top each with 1 teaspoon of strawberry preserves. Place the pastry tops over the preserves and spoon a tablespoon of hot fudge sauce over the top of each. Serve immediately.

NOTE: Assemble only as many puffs as you need. Keep the remaining unfilled puffs covered until ready to use.

Baked Alaska

6 servings

Ah, the chilly, wild freedom of Alaska! Even though this special dessert isn't originally from Alaska, it seems like it should be!

6 single-serving graham cracker tart shells
1 quart chocolate ice cream
2 egg whites
3 tablespoons sugar
$1/8$ teaspoon cream of tartar

Place the tart shells on a cookie sheet and place a medium-sized scoop of chocolate ice cream into each. Cover and place in the freezer. When the shells are completely frozen, preheat the broiler. In a small bowl, with an electric beater on medium speed, beat the egg whites until foamy; continuing to beat, add the sugar and cream of tartar. Beat until stiff peaks form, to make meringue. Remove the ice cream tarts from the freezer and quickly spread the meringue over the ice cream, making sure to cover the ice cream and top edge of crust completely. Place back on the cookie sheet and broil for 2 to 4 minutes, or until the tops are golden. Remove from the broiler and place on another cookie sheet. Cover loosely and freeze for at least 2 hours. When ready to serve, remove from the freezer and allow to stand for 5 minutes.

NOTE: Chocolate ice cream is super here, but you can certainly feel free to use your favorite ice cream or frozen yogurt flavor.

Peanut Sundae Cones

12 cones

It's okay . . . I know that when you were a kid you and your buddies would chase down the ice cream truck just so you could have some of those nutty ice cream cones. I did it, too! Well, now we can make 'em at home any time we want—without having to go running down the street!

12 paper cups (5-ounce size)
1 cup chopped salted peanuts, divided
1 cup (6 ounces) semisweet chocolate chips
2 tablespoons vegetable shortening
1 quart vanilla ice cream
12 sugar cones

Place 1 teaspoon of the nuts in the bottom of each paper cup. In a medium-sized microwave-safe bowl, heat the chocolate and shortening in the microwave on high power for 1 minute. Stir until smooth and completely melted; heat at additional 10-second intervals if needed. Stir the remaining nuts into the melted chocolate, then spoon about 2 teaspoons of the mixture into each cup, enough to come halfway up the side of each cup. Place a scoop of ice cream in a cone and invert the cone into the cup, pressing the ice cream into the chocolate mixture. Repeat with the remaining cones. Freeze the cones (in the cups) for 3 to 4 hours. When ready to serve, just peel the paper off each ice cream cone.

Nutty Snowballs

4 servings

Not only do these taste super, but they're better than the snowballs we make after a new snowfall . . . 'cause we can make them year-round.

1 cup chopped walnuts
¼ cup chocolate sprinkles
1 pint vanilla ice cream
¾ cup hot fudge sauce, warmed

In a small bowl, combine the walnuts and sprinkles; mix well. Place a large scoop of ice cream in the mixture and roll until completely covered, gently pressing the nuts and sprinkles into the ice cream as you roll. Place the ice cream ball on a plate and immediately repeat with the remaining ice cream; freeze for 1 hour, or until firm, then wrap individually in plastic wrap and freeze until ready to serve. To serve, divide the fudge sauce evenly among 4 dessert bowls and place the ice cream balls in the center of the sauce. Serve immediately.

NOTE: Ice cream is a back-to-basics dessert that is truly a favorite of the young and the not-so-young. So if you serve it like this, you're bound to make a big hit!

Family-Sized Sundae

8 to 10 servings

You say your family loves sundaes, but you don't want to make individual sundaes for everyone? Well, if you make this, it's sure to keep them all happy—and full . . . full of "**OOH IT'S SO GOOD!!®**", that is.

½ gallon vanilla ice cream
3 medium-sized bananas, peeled and sliced (about 3 cups)
1 jar (11.75 ounces) hot fudge sauce, warmed
1 container (12 ounces) frozen whipped topping, thawed
½ cup chopped walnuts
⅔ cup maraschino cherries (about 24 cherries)

Scoop half of the ice cream into balls and place the balls in the bottom of a large bowl or trifle dish. Layer with half of the sliced bananas, then spoon ½ cup of the fudge sauce over the bananas. Spread half of the whipped topping over the sauce, then sprinkle on half of the walnuts and half of the cherries; repeat the layers. Cover and freeze for at least 6 hours. Remove from the freezer 10 to 15 minutes before serving.

Cherry Ice Cream Cake

12 to 14 servings

Okay, now I'm gonna show you how to make a delicious ice cream cake like the ones that look so complicated. But guess what—they're not complicated at all! They're easy! You'll see.

1 quart chocolate ice cream, slightly softened
$1\frac{1}{4}$ cups crushed chocolate wafer cookies (about 24 cookies), divided
1 can (17 ounces) pitted dark cherries, drained and patted dry
1 quart strawberry ice cream, slightly softened
1 quart vanilla ice cream, slightly softened

Spread the chocolate ice cream to completely cover the bottom of a 10-inch springform pan. Sprinkle with ½ cup crushed cookies. Place the cherries evenly over the cookies, then cover completely with the strawberry ice cream. Sprinkle ½ cup crushed cookies over the strawberry ice cream, then top with the vanilla ice cream, covering completely. Sprinkle the remaining crushed cookies over the top, cover, and freeze for 3 to 4 hours, or overnight. When ready to serve, remove the springform ring and allow the cake to stand for 10 minutes before slicing into wedges.

NOTE: Make sure you get any remaining cake right back into the freezer after serving.

Ice Cream Pizza

10 to 12 servings

You don't have to be Italian to claim *this* pizza as your own . . . you just have to love serving easy desserts that disappear as soon as you make them!

1 box (21 to 23 ounces) fudge brownie mix, mixed according to the package directions
1 quart vanilla ice cream, slightly softened
½ cup (3 ounces) semisweet chocolate chips
½ cup coarsely chopped walnuts
¼ cup hot fudge sauce, warmed

Preheat the oven to 350°F. Pour the prepared brownie batter into a 12-inch rimmed pizza pan that has been coated with nonstick baking spray. Bake for 16 to 18 minutes, or until a wooden toothpick inserted in the center comes out clean. Remove from the oven and allow to cool completely. Spread the softened ice cream evenly over the top. Sprinkle with the chocolate chips, then with the walnuts. Press the chips and walnuts lightly into the ice cream. Drizzle with the fudge sauce and place in the freezer for 2 to 3 hours, until the ice cream is firm. If freezing for a longer period of time, cover the pizza once the fudge has set. When ready to serve, remove from the freezer and let sit for 5 minutes. Cut into wedges and serve.

Mocha Mud Pie

6 to 8 servings

What? You thought only pigs loved mud?! Wait till you try this chocolate "mud"!

1 pint chocolate ice cream, softened
One prepared 9-inch chocolate pie crust
1 jar (11.75 ounces) hot fudge sauce, warmed, divided
1 pint coffee ice cream, softened
2 tablespoons chopped almonds

Spread the chocolate ice cream in the crust. Cover with about 1 cup of the hot fudge sauce, then cover and freeze for about 2 hours, or until hardened. Spread the coffee ice cream over the frozen pie, then rewarm the remaining fudge sauce and drizzle it over the top. Sprinkle with the almonds, cover, and freeze for at least 2 hours before serving. Remove from the freezer 5 minutes before slicing into wedges.

Creamy Chocolate Pie

6 to 8 servings

We've all heard the saying "as easy as pie." Do you think this recipe is what started it all?

¼ cup unsweetened cocoa
3 tablespoons vegetable oil
¼ cup sugar
⅓ cup milk
4 ounces cream cheese, softened
1 container (8 ounces) frozen whipped topping, thawed
One 9-inch graham cracker pie crust

In a small bowl, stir together the cocoa and oil. Add the sugar and milk and mix with a spoon until smooth. In a large bowl, with an electric beater on medium speed, beat the cream cheese and the cocoa mixture together until smooth. With a spoon, fold the whipped topping into the cream cheese mixture until well blended. Pour into the crust, cover loosely, and freeze for 3 to 4 hours, or until firm. Remove from the freezer 15 minutes before serving.

Cookies 'n' Cream Pie

6 to 8 servings

We all know that Cookies 'n' Cream is a favorite ice cream flavor. Now you can make this special treat at home. It's so quick and easy (and inexpensive) that you'll be making it over and over again!

1 quart vanilla ice cream, softened
12 cream-filled chocolate sandwich cookies, coarsely crushed, divided (see Note)
1 Cookie Pie Crust (page 98), cooled
or
One prepared 9-inch chocolate pie crust

In a medium-sized bowl, combine the ice cream and 1 cup of the crushed cookies; mix well. Spoon the ice cream mixture into the pie crust and top with the remaining crushed cookies. Cover and freeze for at least 3 hours, then remove from the freezer and allow to sit for 5 minutes before serving.

NOTE: The easiest way to crush the cookies is to place them in a resealable plastic storage bag and roll over them gently with a rolling pin. You know, this can be made up to 2 weeks in advance and stored in the freezer, as long as it's well covered.

Chocolate Sherbet

4 servings

When we think of sherbet, we usually think of a frozen fruit dessert. Surprise! This sherbet isn't fruity, it's simply chocolatey! That's what makes it so sinfully delicious!

1/4 cup unsweetened cocoa
6 tablespoons sugar
1/4 cup hot water
1 cup milk
2 tablespoons cold water

In a small saucepan, combine the cocoa and sugar over low heat. Slowly stir in the hot water. Continue stirring over low heat for 2 to 3 minutes, or until the sugar is dissolved and the mixture is warm. Remove from the heat and gradually stir in the milk. Pour into a 7" × 11" baking dish, cover, and freeze for 3 to 4 hours, or until hard. Break up the frozen mixture and place in a food processor that has been fitted with its steel cutting blade or a blender, along with the cold water. Process for 2 to 3 minutes, or until smooth and light-colored. Pour into an airtight container, seal, and freeze for at least 2 hours, or until set.

NOTE: This is one of those recipes where I suggest making a double batch. You know why . . . because it disappears so *fast!*

Chocolate-Dipped Cones

12 cones

Break out your favorite ice cream or frozen yogurt and scoop it into these cones. Watch your gang's eyes light up!

½ cup chopped walnuts
½ cup (3 ounces) semisweet chocolate chips
12 sugar cones

Place the chopped walnuts in a shallow dish. In a small microwave-safe bowl, heat the chocolate in the microwave on high power for 1 minute. Stir the chocolate until it is completely melted; heat at additional 10-second intervals if needed. Hold a cone upside down and dip into the melted chocolate, coating the top edges of the cone. Roll the coated part of the cone in the chopped walnuts. Place the finished cone on waxed paper until the chocolate sets. Repeat with the remaining cones; let cool. Use immediately or store in an airtight container until ready to fill with your favorite ice cream.

My Best Brownies and Bars

Watch them come running when they smell your brownies and bar cookies baking up fresh in the oven!

Cherry Brownies

12 to 15 brownies

With cherries and brownies in every bite, these will give your gang the best of both worlds!

1 box (21 to 23 ounces) brownie mix
2 eggs
¼ cup vegetable oil
1 can (21 ounces) cherry pie filling, divided
2 tablespoons hot water

Preheat the oven to 350°F. In a medium-sized bowl, combine the brownie mix, eggs, oil, and 1 cup of the cherry pie filling; mix well with a spoon. Pour the batter into a 9" × 13" baking dish that has been coated with nonstick baking spray. In a small bowl, combine the hot water and the remaining pie filling and spread evenly over the batter. Bake for 45 to 50 minutes, or until a wooden toothpick inserted in the center comes out clean. Let cool, then cut into squares and serve.

NOTE: You can use regular or extra-fruit pie filling.

S'more Brownies

12 to 15 brownies

If you've ever been camping, you're sure to have made s'mores over an open campfire. Now, with these brownies, you can share the yummy memories of the graham crackers and the melted marshmallows and candy bar. You know they'll keep coming back for s'more!

1 box (21 to 23 ounces) brownie mix, mixed according to the package directions
6 graham crackers, broken into 1-inch chunks
One 5- to 7-ounce milk chocolate candy bar, coarsely chopped
1 cup miniature marshmallows

Preheat the oven to 350°F. Pour the brownie batter into a 9" × 13" baking dish that has been coated with nonstick baking spray. Bake for 15 minutes. Meanwhile, in a medium-sized bowl, combine the remaining ingredients; mix well. Remove the brownies from the oven and sprinkle the marshmallow mixture evenly over the top. Bake for 15 to 20 more minutes, or until a wooden toothpick inserted in the center comes out clean. Cool completely, then cut into squares and serve.

NOTE: If you don't have miniature marshmallows, you can use regular full-sized marshmallows; just cut each into 4 to 6 pieces and use as directed above.

Coffee Brownies

9 to 12 brownies

Wake up your taste buds with the taste that's sweeping the country. Yup, chocolate and coffee is an unbeatable combination that'll really perk you up!

1 cup all-purpose flour
$\frac{1}{2}$ teaspoon baking powder
$\frac{1}{4}$ teaspoon salt
$\frac{1}{3}$ cup warm water
1 tablespoon instant coffee granules
1 cup sugar
$\frac{1}{2}$ cup (1 stick) butter
1 cup (6 ounces) semisweet chocolate chips
3 eggs

Preheat the oven to 350°F. In a small bowl, combine the flour, baking powder, and salt; set aside. In a medium-sized saucepan, combine the water and instant coffee over medium heat; stir until the coffee is completely dissolved. Reduce the heat to low, stir in the sugar and butter, and cook, stirring constantly, until the mixture comes to a boil. Remove the saucepan from the heat and add the chocolate chips, stirring until smooth. Stir in the eggs one at a time, beating well after each addition. Stir in the flour mixture. Pour into an 8-inch square baking pan that has been coated with nonstick baking spray. Bake for 35 to 40 minutes, or until a wooden toothpick inserted in the center comes out clean. Cool in the pan, then cut into squares.

NOTE: Top these with Coffee Frosting (page 171) to make them into Double Coffee Brownies.

Traditional Brownies

9 to 12 brownies

Traditions are so important in families, so I've got another way for you to keep a bit of tradition around your table.

3 squares (1 ounce each) unsweetened chocolate
½ cup (1 stick) butter
1 cup sugar
2 eggs, beaten
⅔ cup all-purpose flour
Pinch of salt
1 teaspoon vanilla extract
1 cup chopped walnuts or other nuts (optional)

Preheat the oven to 350°F. In a double boiler or a medium-sized saucepan, melt the chocolate and butter over low heat. Remove from the heat and transfer to a large bowl. Beat in the sugar and eggs. Stir in the flour, salt, and vanilla until well blended. Stir in the nuts, if using. Pour the batter into an 8-inch square baking pan that has been coated with nonstick baking spray and bake for 30 to 35 minutes, or until the top is dry and almost firm to the touch. Cool in the pan, then cut into squares.

NOTE: For less fudgy brownies, bake them for an additional 5 minutes. If you want to frost these, wait until they're completely cool.

White Macadamia Nut Brownies

12 to 15 brownies

Who says all brownies have to be brown? Not me! I'm sure you'll agree that this will be a pleasant, nutty change of pace.

1 cup (2 sticks) butter, cut into quarters
2 packages (16 ounces each) white baking bars, divided
3/4 cup sugar
1 tablespoon plus 1 teaspoon vanilla extract
4 eggs, lightly beaten
2 cups all-purpose flour
1 jar (7 ounces) macadamia nuts (about 1 1/2 cups), divided

Preheat the oven to 325°F. In a medium-sized saucepan, melt the butter and half of the baking bars over low heat, stirring constantly; remove from the heat and pour into a large bowl. Add the sugar, vanilla, and eggs; beat with an electric beater on medium speed until thoroughly mixed. (The mixture may appear curdled.) Add the flour and mix until well combined. Coarsely chop the remaining baking bars into chunks and add to the batter along with 1 cup of the nuts. Pour the batter into a 9" × 13" baking dish that has been coated with nonstick baking spray. Top with the remaining nuts. Bake for 30 to 35 minutes, or until golden. Cool and cut into squares.

NOTE: If you prefer to use smaller nut pieces in your brownies, cut them in half or coarsely chop them, being careful not to make them too small. Roasted almonds will also work well if you'd rather use them than macadamias. (See page 147 for roasting instructions.)

French Brownies

12 to 15 brownies

The French have a classic dessert that combines flavorful raspberries with the big taste of chocolate. I've got a shortcut approach that'll give you the same big taste with just a small bit of work.

1 package (21 to 23 ounces) brownie mix, mixed according to the package directions
3/4 cup (4 1/2 ounces) semisweet chocolate chips
3/4 cup raspberry preserves, divided

Preheat the oven to 350°F. Place the brownie batter in a large bowl; stir in the chocolate chips and 1/2 cup of the raspberry preserves. Pour into a 9" × 13" baking dish that has been coated with nonstick baking spray. Bake for 25 to 30 minutes, or until a wooden toothpick inserted in the center comes out clean. Let cool for 20 minutes, then spread the remaining raspberry preserves over the top. Cut into bars and serve.

NOTE: Some people prefer seedless raspberry preserves and others prefer preserves with seeds. The choice is yours.

Butterscotch Coconut Brownies

15 to 18 brownies

Rich? Of course! Gooey? You bet! So make sure you have a big glass of ice-cold milk on hand to wash them down.

½ cup (3 ounces) semisweet chocolate chips
½ cup (3 ounces) butterscotch chips
½ cup shredded coconut
1 package (21 to 23 ounces) brownie mix, mixed according to the package directions

Preheat the oven to 350°F. In a medium-sized bowl, combine the chocolate chips, butterscotch chips, and coconut; mix well and set aside. Place the brownie batter in a large bowl. Stir in half of the chip mixture, then pour into a 9" × 13" baking dish that has been coated with nonstick baking spray. Sprinkle the remaining chip mixture over the top and bake for 25 to 30 minutes, or until a wooden toothpick inserted in the center comes out clean. Allow to cool, then cut into bars.

NOTE: You'll probably have some open packages of chips on hand after making these—be sure to store them in airtight containers to keep them fresh.

Chocolate–Peanut Butter Brownies

9 to 12 brownies

I know this recipe says to cool before cutting, but my grandchildren can never wait that long! They love 'em right out of the oven.

½ cup creamy or crunchy peanut butter
¼ cup (½ stick) butter, softened
1 cup firmly packed light brown sugar
2 eggs
1 teaspoon vanilla extract
1 cup self-rising flour
1 cup (6 ounces) semisweet chocolate chips

Preheat the oven to 300°F. In a medium-sized bowl, with an electric beater on medium speed, beat the peanut butter, butter, and brown sugar until light and fluffy. Add the eggs one at a time, beating well after each addition. Blend in the vanilla, then beat in the flour. Fold in the chocolate chips until well combined. Spread the batter evenly in an 8-inch square baking pan that has been coated with nonstick baking spray. Bake for 45 to 50 minutes, or until golden. Remove from the oven and place the pan on a wire rack. Allow to cool completely before cutting.

Hot Fudge Brownies à la Mode

6 to 9 servings

When I was a kid, I thought that *à la mode* was a really fancy name . . . that is, until I found out it simply means something served with ice cream. Well, most of us love ice cream, so no matter what we call this, it's bound to be one of our favorites.

1 cup all-purpose flour
3/4 cup granulated sugar
1/4 cup plus 2 tablespoons unsweetened cocoa, divided
2 teaspoons baking powder
1/2 teaspoon salt
1/2 cup milk
2 tablespoons vegetable oil
1 teaspoon vanilla extract
3/4 cup chopped walnuts
3/4 cup firmly packed dark or light brown sugar
1 3/4 cups hot water
1 quart vanilla ice cream

Preheat the oven to 350°F. In a large bowl, combine the flour, granulated sugar, 2 tablespoons cocoa, baking powder, and salt. Add the milk, oil, and vanilla; mix with a spoon until smooth. Stir in the walnuts and pour the batter into an 8-inch square baking pan that has been coated with nonstick baking spray. In a small bowl, combine the brown sugar and remaining cocoa; sprinkle evenly over the batter. Pour the hot water over the brown sugar and cocoa. Bake for 35 to 40 minutes, or until the top is cracked and the brownies are just firm to the touch. Remove from the oven and let cool for 15 minutes. Cut into squares and place on individual serving plates. Top each with a scoop of ice cream and the fudge sauce from the bottom of the pan.

Pecan Fudgies

18 bars

If you have a cookie jar that needs filling, I recommend these. But I can't guarantee how long they'll stay in there!

2½ cups all-purpose flour
2 cups sugar
¾ cup unsweetened cocoa
1 teaspoon baking soda
1 teaspoon salt
⅔ cup vegetable oil
1 teaspoon vanilla extract
1½ cups cold water
2 eggs
1 cup (6 ounces) semisweet chocolate chips
1 cup chopped pecans

Preheat the oven to 350°F. In a large bowl, combine all the ingredients except the chocolate chips and pecans; mix until well blended. Pour into a greased and floured 9" × 13" baking pan. Sprinkle the chocolate chips and pecans over the top. Bake for 40 to 45 minutes, or until a wooden toothpick inserted in the center comes out clean. Cool, then cut into bars.

Apple Chip Squares

12 to 15 squares

When I lived in Upstate New York, I had a friend who had some apple trees in her yard. Every year she turned those apples into a luscious autumn apple treat. Now I'm taking her recipe a step further by adding some chocolate chips . . . and, believe me, it's become a year-round favorite at my house!

1¾ cups all-purpose flour
1 cup sugar
½ teaspoon baking soda
½ teaspoon salt
2 eggs
½ cup vegetable oil
¼ cup apple juice
1 teaspoon vanilla extract
2 medium-sized tart apples, peeled, cored, and coarsely chopped
1 cup (6 ounces) semisweet chocolate chips
½ cup chopped walnuts

Preheat the oven to 350°F. In a large bowl, combine the flour, sugar, baking soda, and salt; mix well. With an electric beater, beat in the eggs, oil, apple juice, and vanilla until well blended. With a spoon, fold in the apples, chocolate chips, and nuts. Pour into a 9" × 13" baking dish that has been coated with nonstick baking spray. Bake for 40 to 45 minutes, or until a wooden toothpick inserted in the center comes out clean. Allow to cool, then cut into squares and serve.

Five-Layer Bars

20 to 24 bars

These bars have five fantastic layers of fabulous flavor. See if you can taste each one!

1½ cups graham cracker crumbs
½ cup (1 stick) butter, melted
1 can (14 ounces) sweetened condensed milk
1 cup raisins
1 cup (6 ounces) semisweet chocolate chips
½ cup chopped walnuts
½ cup shredded coconut

Preheat the oven to 350°F. In a medium-sized bowl, combine the graham cracker crumbs and butter; mix well and press into a 9" × 13" baking dish that has been coated with nonstick baking spray. Pour the sweetened condensed milk evenly over the crumb mixture, then sprinkle evenly with the raisins, chocolate chips, nuts, and coconut. Bake for 25 to 30 minutes, or until lightly browned. Cool for 10 minutes, then chill for 30 minutes. Cut into bars and serve.

NOTE: These freeze well, so why not make two batches, so you can have one now and one on hand for unexpected company—or for another treat for the family.

Chocolate Ruby Treasures

12 to 15 squares

No real rubies are required to make these . . . just maraschino cherries that end up looking like rubies but tasting scrumptious in these moist squares. (And you thought diamonds were a girl's best friend!)

2 cups all-purpose flour
½ teaspoon baking powder
½ teaspoon baking soda
½ teaspoon salt
½ cup granulated sugar
½ cup firmly packed light or dark brown sugar
½ cup (1 stick) butter, softened
2 eggs
1 teaspoon vanilla extract
1 cup milk
1 cup chopped walnuts
1 cup (6 ounces) semisweet chocolate chips
1 jar (16 ounces) maraschino cherries, drained and coarsely chopped

Preheat the oven to 325°F. In a medium-sized bowl, combine the flour, baking powder, baking soda, and salt; mix well and set aside. In a large bowl, with an electric beater on high speed, beat together the granulated sugar, brown sugar, and butter until creamy. Add the eggs and vanilla and continue beating until blended, then add the milk and blend well. Gradually add the flour mixture and beat until well mixed. With a spoon, stir in the remaining ingredients. Pour into a 9" × 13" baking dish that has been coated with nonstick baking spray. Bake for 35 to 40 minutes, or until the top is light golden and a wooden toothpick inserted in the center comes out clean. Let cool completely before cutting into bars.

Chocolate Takes the Cake

From layer cake to babka to
awesome éclair cake,
chocolate cake fits any occasion!

Batter Up!

In this chapter you're going to find all kinds of chocolate cake options. And here's an extra big one that I want to share: Say you want to make a layer cake and you've chosen a recipe that gives only the directions for using a 9" × 13" pan. Or you want to make a 9" × 13" cake from a batter that I've given as a Bundt cake? That's easy! I've marked the pages with a where you can make pan changes without changing the batter instructions. Changing the pan might also require a change in the baking time, so when you see this symbol , you'll know you can make the following adjustments:

The same batter can be baked in:	Or:	Baking time change:
9" × 13" baking pan	Two 8-inch round layer pans	Same baking time
Bundt pan	A 9" × 13" baking pan	About 5 minutes more in a Bundt pan than a 9" × 13" pan
Two 9-inch round layer pans	• A 9" × 13" baking pan • Two 8-inch round layer pans (will be thicker than the 9-inch layers)	About 5 minutes less in two 9-inch pans
9" × 13" baking pan	About 24 muffin cups	About 10 minutes less for muffins

Note: This guide is for use with the cakes in this chapter that have the key.

Good Ol' Chocolate Cake

10 to 12 servings

There's nothing like a good ol' chocolate cake to put everybody in a good mood.

2/3 cup milk
2 tablespoons white vinegar
1 cup water
1/2 cup (1 stick) butter
3 squares (1 ounce each) unsweetened chocolate
2 cups sugar
2 cups all-purpose flour
1 1/2 teaspoons baking soda
1/4 teaspoon salt
2 eggs, beaten

Preheat the oven to 350°F. In a small bowl, combine the milk and vinegar; mix well, then set aside for 10 minutes, until thickened. Meanwhile, in a medium-sized saucepan, combine the water and butter over medium-high heat; bring to a boil, then remove from the heat and stir in the chocolate until it is completely melted. In a large bowl, combine the remaining ingredients except the eggs. Add the chocolate mixture to the large bowl and blend with an electric beater on medium speed until well mixed. Add the milk mixture, then gradually add the eggs, continuing to beat until the mixture is well blended. Pour into a 9" × 13" baking pan that has been coated with nonstick baking spray. Bake for 25 to 30 minutes, or until a wooden toothpick inserted in the center comes out clean. If planning to frost the cake, let cool slightly, then invert onto a wire rack to cool completely. If planning to serve plain, invert the cake onto another rack to cool completely before serving.

See page 65 for directions on using a different-size pan.

Chocolate Mayonnaise Cake

10 to 12 servings

I know you may not believe what you read when you see that there's mayonnaise in here . . . yup, mayonnaise! But, after all, what *is* mayonnaise, anyway, but eggs and oil. That's what makes this cake so moist and rich—just like the cake that everybody's mom used to make for birthday parties (and just the way we all *still* like it)!

2 cups all-purpose flour
1 cup sugar
2 teaspoons baking soda
1/4 cup unsweetened cocoa
1 cup mayonnaise
1 cup water
1 teaspoon vanilla extract
Buttercream Frosting (page 169)

Preheat the oven to 350°F. In a large bowl, combine all the cake ingredients and blend with an electric beater on medium speed; mix well. Divide the batter between two 8-inch round cake pans that have been coated with nonstick baking spray and lightly floured. Bake for 20 to 25 minutes, or until a wooden toothpick inserted in the center comes out clean. Let cool for 15 minutes, then invert onto racks to cool completely. Meanwhile, prepare the Buttercream Frosting. Place one cake layer upside down on a serving plate and frost the top. Place the second layer over the first and frost the top and sides. Slice and serve.

NOTE: If you freeze the cake a bit before frosting, it will make the job easier and neater. And for a real chocolate-lover's delight, frost with Chocolate Frosting (page 168) instead of buttercream.

See page 65 for directions on using a different-size pan.

Shortcut German Chocolate Cake

12 to 15 servings

The taste of a European pastry shop, with the ease of a packaged cake mix. Yeah, really!

1 package (18.25 ounces) chocolate cake mix, mixed according to the package directions
1 cup chopped pecans, divided
1 cup shredded coconut, divided
1 cup sweetened condensed milk
3 tablespoons butter
1 teaspoon vanilla extract

Preheat the oven to 350°F. Place the cake batter in a large bowl and add ½ cup of the pecans and ½ cup of the coconut; mix well. Pour into a 9" × 13" baking pan that has been coated with nonstick baking spray and floured. Bake for 30 to 35 minutes, or until a wooden toothpick inserted in the center comes out clean. In a small saucepan, combine the sweetened condensed milk, butter, and vanilla over medium heat. Cook for about 5 minutes, until thickened, stirring constantly. Stir in the remaining ½ cup pecans and ½ cup coconut. Spread over the warm cake and allow the cake to cool completely before cutting into squares.

See page 65 for directions on using a different-size pan.

Rocky Road Bundt Cake

10 to 12 servings

I've got a mathematical equation that really adds up: Chocolate plus walnuts plus marshmallow equals Rocky Road heaven. Now that's my kind of addition!

1 package (18.25 ounces) chocolate cake mix, mixed according to the package directions
½ cup plus 2 tablespoons miniature semisweet chocolate chips, divided
½ cup plus 2 tablespoons chopped walnuts, divided
½ cup marshmallow creme

Preheat the oven to 350°F. Place the cake batter in a large bowl and stir in ½ cup chocolate chips and ½ cup walnuts. Pour into a 10-inch Bundt or tube pan that has been coated with nonstick baking spray and lightly floured. Bake for 45 to 50 minutes, or until a wooden toothpick inserted in the center comes out clean. Remove from the oven and let cool for about 20 minutes. Invert the cake onto a wire cooling rack and remove the pan; cool thoroughly. Place the cake on a serving platter when cooled. In a small saucepan, melt the marshmallow creme over low heat, stirring constantly. Pour over the cake and top with the remaining 2 tablespoons each chocolate chips and walnuts.

See page 65 for directions on using a different-size pan.

Banana Chocolate Swirl Cake

9 to 12 servings

Chocolate swirled into sweet banana cake . . . doesn't that sound like something you've just gotta make right now?! Bye. . . .

1 cup sugar
½ cup vegetable shortening
2 eggs
2 cups all-purpose flour
1 teaspoon baking soda
½ teaspoon salt
1 cup mashed ripe bananas (about 3 bananas)
1 teaspoon vanilla extract
1 cup (6 ounces) semisweet chocolate chips, melted

Preheat the oven to 350°F. In a large bowl, with an electric beater on medium speed, cream the sugar and shortening until light and fluffy. Add the eggs and beat thoroughly. Slowly blend in the flour, baking soda, and salt. Beat in the mashed bananas and the vanilla until well mixed. Pour half the batter into a 7" × 11" baking pan that has been coated with nonstick baking spray. Pour half of the melted chocolate over the batter. Pour on the remaining batter, then the remaining chocolate. With a knife, swirl the chocolate through the batter. Bake for 40 to 45 minutes, or until a wooden toothpick inserted in the center comes out clean. Allow to cool, then cut into squares.

Fudgy Pistachio Cake

10 to 12 servings

I already know how much you love chocolate. If you love the flavor of pistachio, too, then this is the cake for you! And since it calls for a cake mix and a pudding mix, you'll be enjoying it in no time!

1 package (18.25 ounces) white cake mix
1 package (4-serving size) instant pistachio pudding and pie filling
4 eggs
1 cup water
1/3 cup vegetable oil
1/2 cup miniature candy-coated chocolate baking bits
1/4 cup shelled pistachio nuts, chopped

Preheat the oven to 350°F. In a large bowl, with an electric beater on medium speed, beat the cake and pudding mixes, eggs, water, and oil for about 2 minutes, until thoroughly mixed. With a spoon, stir in the chocolate bits and nuts. Pour the batter into a 10-inch Bundt pan that has been coated with nonstick baking spray and floured. Bake for 55 to 60 minutes, or until a wooden toothpick inserted in the center comes out clean. Cool in the pan for 25 to 30 minutes, then invert onto a wire rack to cool completely.

NOTE: Before your family "finishes it off," you might want to "finish off" the cake by drizzling the top of the cooled cake with Chocolate Glaze (page 174) or confectioners' sugar. If you can't find the miniature candy-coated chocolate bits, full-sized ones will work just as well.

See page 65 for directions on using a different-size pan.

Chocolate Snack Cake

12 to 15 servings

You parents out there often have your hands full—I know, 'cause my wife, Ethel, and I raised three kids! And I know just what you need—something to take to the bake sale, or the Scout meeting, or to the PTA function. Well, here it is, just the right snack for you to make and take anywhere!

3 cups all-purpose flour
2 cups sugar
$\frac{1}{2}$ cup unsweetened cocoa
2 teaspoons baking soda
1 teaspoon salt
2 cups black coffee
$\frac{2}{3}$ cup vegetable oil
2 tablespoons vinegar
2 teaspoons vanilla extract

Preheat the oven to 350°F. In a 9" × 13" baking dish, combine the flour, sugar, cocoa, baking soda, and salt. Add the coffee, oil, vinegar, and vanilla. Stir until the batter is a uniform color throughout. Bake for 30 to 35 minutes, or until a wooden toothpick inserted in the center comes out clean. Cool completely, then cut into squares and off you go!

NOTE: I love to top this cake with Caramel Frosting (page 172), but you don't have to limit yourself to that. If there's another one that you prefer, use it, or you could simply sprinkle the cooled cake with confectioners' sugar!

See page 65 for directions on using a different-size pan.

Pirates' Cove Cake

10 to 12 servings

In adventure stories, the traditional drink of pirates is rum, so I made this special chocolate rum cake and named it for them. And you'd better watch out, matey, 'cause you might have to walk the plank if you don't make this often enough for your crew!

1 box (18.5 ounces) chocolate cake mix
1 package (4-serving size) instant chocolate pudding and pie filling
½ cup sour cream
½ cup vegetable oil
4 eggs
½ cup light rum
½ cup strong black coffee
2 cups (12 ounces) semisweet chocolate chips
Quick Rum Glaze (page 175)

Preheat the oven to 350°F. In a large bowl, combine the cake and pudding mixes, sour cream, oil, and eggs; beat well with an electric beater. Beat in the rum and coffee, then, with a spoon, stir in the chocolate chips. Pour the batter into a 10-inch Bundt pan that has been coated with nonstick baking spray and lightly floured. Bake for 50 to 55 minutes, or until a wooden toothpick inserted in the center comes out clean. Let cool for 20 to 25 minutes, then invert the cake onto a serving plate. Prepare the rum glaze and drizzle it over the cooled cake.

See page 65 for directions on using a different-size pan.

Cherry Almond Upside-Down Cake

12 to 15 servings

Move over, pineapple upside-down cake! Everybody's gonna be head over heels for the new cake in town.

1 cup drained and chopped maraschino cherries
½ cup sliced or slivered almonds
1 package (18.25 ounces) chocolate cake mix, mixed according to the package directions
4 ounces cream cheese, softened
¼ cup (½ stick) butter, melted
1 cup confectioners' sugar

Preheat the oven to 350°F. Spread the cherries evenly over the bottom of a 9" × 13" baking dish that has been coated with nonstick baking spray and floured. Sprinkle the almonds over the cherries, then pour the prepared cake batter over the cherries and almonds. In a medium-sized bowl, combine the cream cheese and melted butter and beat with an electric beater until creamy. Add the sugar and beat until smooth. Starting 1 inch from the edge of the baking dish, drop the mixture in 12 equal spoonfuls evenly over the cake batter, pushing the cream cheese mixture into the batter. Bake for 45 to 50 minutes, or until a wooden toothpick inserted in the center comes out clean. Cool for 25 to 30 minutes, then invert onto a platter; cut and serve when completely cooled.

NOTE: To bring out the flavor of the almonds, lightly toast them in a 350°F. oven for a few minutes before using as directed.

See page 65 for directions on using a different-size pan.

Chocolate Orange Swirl Cake

10 to 12 servings

Don't bother looking for chocolate syrup to put on top of your cake . . . it's already mixed in!

1 cup (2 sticks) butter, softened
2 cups granulated sugar
1 tablespoon orange extract or grated zest of 1 orange
3 eggs
2¾ cups all-purpose flour
1¼ teaspoons baking soda, divided
½ teaspoon salt
1 cup sour cream
1 cup chocolate-flavored syrup
1 teaspoon confectioners' sugar (optional)

Preheat the oven to 350°F. In a large bowl, with an electric beater on medium speed, cream the butter, granulated sugar, and orange extract until light and fluffy. Add the eggs and beat well. In another large bowl, combine the flour, 1 teaspoon baking soda, and salt. Add alternately in several additions with the sour cream to the butter mixture, beating until well mixed. In a medium-sized bowl, combine the syrup and the remaining ¼ teaspoon baking soda. Add 2 cups of the batter to the syrup mixture and mix well; set aside. Pour the remaining batter into a 10-inch Bundt pan that has been coated with nonstick baking spray and lightly floured. Pour the chocolate batter over the top of the yellow batter. Do not mix. Bake for 65 to 70 minutes, or until a wooden toothpick inserted in the center comes out clean. Cool for 15 minutes, then remove from the pan and cool completely. Sprinkle the cooled cake with the confectioners' sugar, if desired.

See page 65 for directions on using a different-size pan.

Banana Bungalow

10 to 12 servings

When you think of a bungalow, you think of a little cottage that's homey and comfortable, don't you? Well, it's easy to build my version of a dessert bungalow. It'll give you a homey, comfortable feeling with every bite.

1 package (18.25 ounces) chocolate cake mix, mixed according to the package directions
1 container (16 ounces) frozen whipped topping, thawed, divided
3 large bananas, peeled
2 tablespoons chocolate sprinkles

Preheat the oven to 350°F. Pour the prepared cake batter into a 10" × 15" rimmed baking sheet or jelly-roll pan that has been coated with nonstick baking spray and lightly floured. Bake for 22 to 24 minutes, or until a wooden toothpick inserted in the center comes out clean. Allow to cool, then invert onto a large platter. Cut crosswise into 3 sections, each measuring 5" × 10", as shown in illustration 1 on the opposite page. Reserve 1 cup whipped topping for the frosting. Spread some of the remaining whipped topping over the middle section of cake, completely covering it. Lay 2 bananas parallel to each other over the whipped topping. Spoon more whipped topping over the bananas, then place the third banana on top. Cover with the remaining whipped topping, as shown in illustration 2 on the opposite page. Gently bring up the 2 side pieces of cake from the outer edges to form the bungalow roof. Frost the cake with the reserved whipped topping, then cover with the sprinkles, as shown in illustration 3 on the opposite page. Refrigerate for at least 1 hour, then slice and serve.

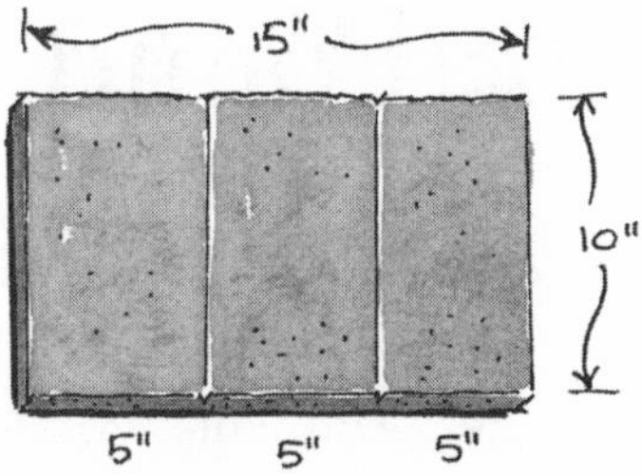

1

2

3

Chocolate Pound Cake

2 loaf cakes, 8 to 10 servings each

Who doesn't love pound cake?! And when you taste this chocolate version, you're gonna love it even more!

1½ cups (3 sticks) butter, softened
5 eggs
3 cups sugar
½ cup unsweetened cocoa
1 teaspoon vanilla extract
3 cups all-purpose flour
1 cup milk

In a large bowl, with an electric beater on medium speed, beat the butter until fluffy. Alternately add the eggs (one at a time) and the sugar (1 cup at a time), beating well after each addition. Add the cocoa and vanilla; blend well. Alternately add the flour and milk, blending well and ending with flour. Scrape down the sides of the bowl and continue beating until well mixed. Pour the batter into two 9" × 5" loaf pans that have been coated with nonstick baking spray and lightly floured. Place the plans on a rack in the center of a cold oven. Set the temperature to 300°F. and bake for 80 to 90 minutes, or until a wooden toothpick inserted in the center comes out clean. Cool in pans for about 30 minutes, then remove to platters.

NOTE: Serve slices of this on a pool of Vanilla Sauce (page 164) with fresh strawberries. If you'd like, enjoy one cake now and freeze the second one for later.

Seven-Layer Cake

8 to 10 servings

Did you look at this title and think, "No way am I going to the trouble of making a cake with seven layers!"? Well, stay with me while I explain that you use a prepared pound cake. Now what do you think? Believe me, it's worth a shot!

½ cup (1 stick) butter
2 cups (12 ounces) semisweet chocolate chips
¼ cup confectioners' sugar
One 13- to 16-ounce frozen pound cake
2 tablespoons chopped walnuts

In a medium-sized saucepan, melt the butter and chocolate chips over medium heat, stirring constantly until smooth. Remove from the heat and add the confectioners' sugar 1 tablespoon at a time, stirring thoroughly after each addition. With a serrated knife, carefully slice the frozen cake into 7 *horizontal* slices. Reserve ½ cup of the chocolate sauce for frosting the sides of the cake. Place bottom slice on a platter and spread 2 tablespoons of the remaining sauce over the slice. Place the second slice over the first, and spread with 2 tablespoons chocolate sauce. Repeat with the remaining layers and sauce. Spread the sides with the reserved sauce and evenly sprinkle the top with the nuts. Slice and serve.

NOTE: If you want, go all chocolate and use a frozen chocolate pound cake.

Quick Boston Cream Cake

8 to 10 servings

No, it's not a misprint, I really do mean *cake,* not pie! This one closes in on the tastes of the original New England favorite, but it's easier . . . *and* you can still say you made it yourself!

1 package (4-serving size) instant vanilla pudding and pie filling
1 cup cold milk
One 13- to 16-ounce frozen pound cake, thawed
½ cup (3 ounces) semisweet chocolate chips
1 tablespoon water

In a medium-sized bowl, with an electric beater on medium speed, beat the pudding mix and milk for 1 to 2 minutes, until the pudding begins to thicken. Slice the pound cake in half horizontally. Place the bottom half of the pound cake on a serving plate and spread the pudding evenly over the cake. Place the top half of the cake over the pudding. In a small microwave-safe bowl, combine the chocolate chips and water. Heat in the microwave on high power for 30 to 45 seconds to melt the chocolate; stir until smooth. With a spoon, spread the chocolate over the top of the cake and allow to drip down the sides. Serve immediately, or cover and chill until ready to serve.

NOTE: The chocolate chips can also be melted in a saucepan over low heat or in a double boiler over warm water, but stir constantly and watch carefully so the chocolate doesn't burn.

Chocolate Hazelnut "Torte"

8 to 10 servings

No mistakes here . . . it really *is* a breeze to make this delicious favorite!

One (13- to 16-ounce) frozen pound cake
1 jar (13 ounces) chocolate hazelnut spread

Slice the frozen pound cake into 4 horizontal layers. Place the bottom cake layer on a serving plate. Spread with a thin layer of the chocolate hazelnut spread, then place another cake layer on top. Repeat with the remaining layers and more spread. Frost the top and sides of the cake with the remaining chocolate hazelnut spread. Chill for 3 to 4 hours, or until the chocolate hazelnut spread is firm. Slice and serve.

NOTE: Chocolate hazelnut spread can usually be found alongside the peanut butter in most supermarkets. You know, you can make this in advance and freeze it until needed. Just place the cake in the freezer long enough to freeze the hazelnut spread, then remove the cake, wrap tightly in plastic wrap and then aluminum foil, and return it to the freezer. When ready to use, unwrap the cake and allow it to thaw in the refrigerator overnight.

Chocolate Babka

10 to 12 servings

You won't believe the raves you'll get from this simple, delicious recipe. In fact, I'm sure it'll become one of your all-time favorites in no time flat!

½ cup (3 ounces) semisweet chocolate chips, chopped
⅓ cup chopped walnuts
⅓ cup firmly packed light brown sugar
1 large package (17.3 ounces) refrigerated buttermilk biscuits (8 biscuits)
1 small package (10.8 ounces) refrigerated buttermilk biscuits (5 biscuits)
1 tablespoon butter, melted

Preheat the oven to 350°F. In a small bowl, combine the chocolate chips, walnuts, and brown sugar; mix well. Lay out the 13 biscuits on a clean, smooth surface. Cut each biscuit into 6 pieces and place in a large bowl. Pour the melted butter over the biscuit pieces. Sprinkle the chocolate chip mixture over the biscuit pieces, then toss until evenly coated. Place the dough in a 10-inch Bundt pan that has been coated with nonstick baking spray. Bake for 25 to 30 minutes, or until the center is firm. Let cool for 10 to 15 minutes, then invert the Bundt pan over a plate to remove the cake from the pan.

NOTE: To save a step, you could use whole miniature chocolate chips instead of the chopped chocolate chips.

Heavenly Surprise Angel Cake

10 to 12 servings

Yup, it's true! You'll think you're in heaven when you try this delicious cake. And you've got to watch people's faces when you slice it . . . they'll be trying to figure out how you stuffed it!

1 envelope (0.25 ounce) unflavored gelatin
¼ cup cold water
One 10-inch prepared angel food cake
1½ cups heavy cream
⅔ cup sugar
⅓ cup unsweetened cocoa
2 teaspoons vanilla extract

In a small microwave-safe bowl, sprinkle the gelatin over the water; let stand for 2 minutes. Heat in the microwave on high power for 40 seconds, then stir thoroughly until the gelatin is completely dissolved. Let stand until cool and slightly thickened. Meanwhile, place the cake on a serving plate. Cut a 1-inch horizontal layer off the top of the cake, as shown in illustration 1 on the opposite page; set aside the top. Without cutting through the bottom of the cake, make a vertical cut ½ inch from the outside edge of the cake all the way around the cake, then make another vertical cut (parallel to the first one) ½ inch from the inside edge of the cake all around the cake, as shown in illustration 2 on the opposite page. Gently remove the cake between the 2 cuts, forming a trench, being careful not to tear the bottom of the cake; reserve it for another use. In a medium-sized bowl, with an electric beater on medium speed, beat the cream until soft peaks form. Gradually add the sugar and cocoa and continue beating until the mixture forms stiff peaks. Beat in the gelatin and vanilla. Spoon enough of the mixture into the hollowed-out cake to fill it and replace the top layer. Frost the cake with the remaining chocolate mixture, as shown in illustration 3 below. Refrigerate for at least 1 hour before serving.

NOTE: You won't have to worry about using the cake that came out of the center; put it out for your little angels and watch it disappear!

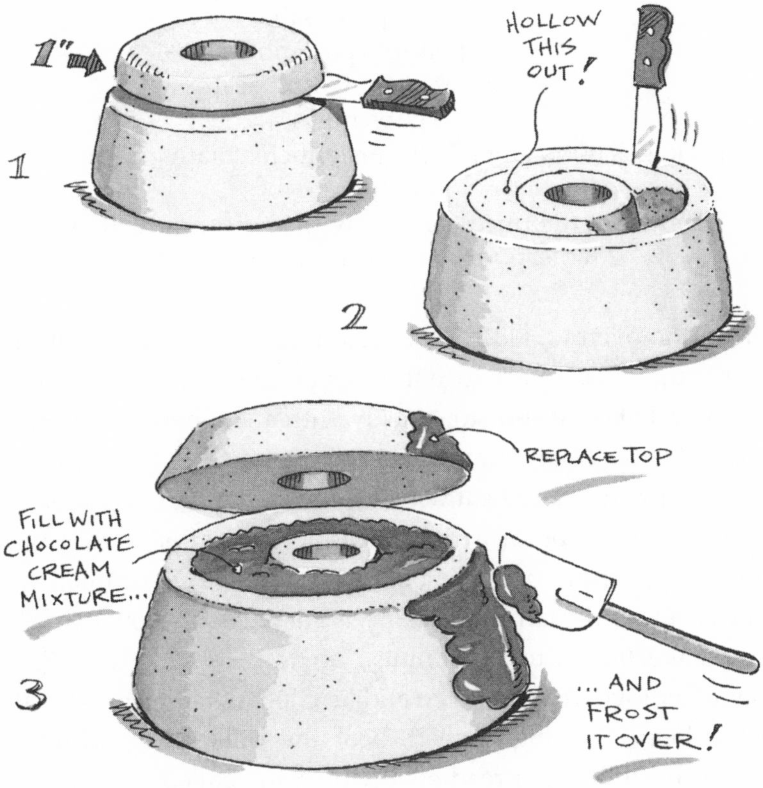

Éclair Cake

10 to 12 servings

Éclairs always look so beautiful in pastry shop windows. And they look like they'd be pretty complicated to make, too. Fortunately, one of my viewers shared a secret with me about how to get those same tastes in a light cake. Give it a whirl!

1 cup water
½ cup (1 stick) butter, cut into quarters
¼ teaspoon salt
1 cup all-purpose flour
4 eggs, at room temperature
3 cups milk
2 packages (4 servings each) instant chocolate pudding and pie filling
1 container (8 ounces) frozen whipped topping, thawed
2 tablespoons chocolate-flavored syrup

Preheat the oven to 400°F. In a medium-sized saucepan, bring the water, butter, and salt to a boil over medium-high heat. Add the flour all at once and stir quickly with a wooden spoon until the mixture forms a ball; remove the saucepan from the heat. Add 1 egg to the mixture and beat with a wooden spoon to blend. Add the remaining eggs one at a time, beating well after each addition. Spread the mixture over the bottom of a 10" × 15" rimmed cookie sheet or jelly-roll pan that has been coated with nonstick baking spray. Bake for 20 to 25 minutes, or until the edges are golden brown. Remove from the oven and let cool. In a large bowl, with an electric beater on high speed, beat the milk and pudding mix together until thick. Spread evenly over the baked shell, then chill for 1 hour. Just before serving, spread the whipped topping over the chocolate pudding and drizzle with the chocolate syrup.

Flourless Chocolate Cake

12 to 16 servings

That's right—a cake with no flour. That's your first surprise. The second is how rich it is (so slice thin pieces!). Hey, maybe I should have called it Double Surprise Cake.

2 cups (12 ounces) semisweet chocolate chips
½ cup (1 stick) butter
¼ cup sugar
¼ cup water
1 teaspoon instant coffee granules
3 eggs
Whipped Cream (page 176)

Preheat the oven to 425°F. Butter the bottom and sides of a 9-inch pie plate. Place a 12" × 12" sheet of waxed paper in the plate and butter the waxed paper. In a medium-sized saucepan, combine the chocolate chips, butter, sugar, water, and coffee granules and heat over medium heat for 2 to 3 minutes, until the chocolate and butter are melted, stirring constantly. Remove from the heat and stir in the eggs until the mixture is smooth. Pour into the waxed paper–lined pie plate. Bake for 10 minutes; the cake will not be completely set in the middle. Cool, cover loosely, then chill for 6 to 8 hours, or overnight. When ready to serve, remove the cake from the refrigerator and allow to sit for 10 minutes. Prepare the whipped cream, then invert the cake onto a large flat serving dish and remove the waxed paper. Top with the whipped cream.

Chocolate Swirl Cheesecake

12 to 16 servings

Imagine being the hit of a potluck supper or even the neighborhood coffee klatch. Whip up one of these—and get ready for all the raves.

2 cups graham cracker crumbs
½ cup (1 stick) butter, melted
1¼ cups plus 2 tablespoons sugar, divided
3 packages (8 ounces each) cream cheese, softened
4 eggs
2 teaspoons vanilla extract, divided
1 cup (6 ounces) miniature semisweet chocolate chips
1 container (16 ounces) sour cream
1 tablespoon unsweetened cocoa

Preheat the oven to 350°F. In a medium-sized bowl, combine the graham cracker crumbs, butter, and 2 tablespoons sugar; mix well. Press into a 10-inch springform pan, covering the bottom and sides. Chill while preparing the filling. In a large bowl, blend the cream cheese and 1 cup sugar with an electric beater. Add the eggs one at a time, beating well after each addition, then add 1 teaspoon vanilla; mix well. With a spoon, stir in the chocolate chips. Pour the filling into the chilled crust and bake for 55 to 60 minutes, or until firm. Remove from the oven and let cool for 5 minutes. (Leave the oven on.) Meanwhile, in a medium-sized bowl, with a spoon, mix the sour cream and the remaining sugar and vanilla until well combined. Carefully spread 1½ cups of the sour cream mixture over the top of the cheesecake. Mix the remaining sour cream mixture with the cocoa and drizzle over the top. Swirl with a knife and bake for 5 more minutes. Let cool, then refrigerate overnight before serving.

Miniature Chocolate Cheesecakes

24 miniature cheesecakes

Cheesecake is a particular weakness of mine—it's hard for me to say no when it's offered to me, especially chocolate cheesecake. You won't be able to say no to these special miniature cheesecakes either, 'cause they're so rich and yummy.

24 vanilla wafer cookies
3 packages (8 ounces each) cream cheese, softened
1/2 cup unsweetened cocoa
1/4 cup (1/2 stick) butter, melted
2 teaspoons vanilla extract
1 can (14 ounces) sweetened condensed milk
3 eggs

Preheat the oven to 300°F. Line 24 regular-sized muffin cups with paper baking cups. Place a vanilla wafer in the bottom of each paper cup. In a large bowl, with an electric beater on medium speed, beat the cream cheese until creamy. Add the cocoa, butter, and vanilla, beating until well blended. Slowly add the sweetened condensed milk, then the eggs, beating until thoroughly mixed. Spoon into the baking cups and bake for 30 to 35 minutes, or until set. Cool completely, then refrigerate until ready to serve.

NOTE: Why not top these with an assortment of toppings—from canned pie filling to sliced fresh fruit to fresh Whipped Cream (page 176)? Go ahead. Have a ball!

Fudge-Filled Cupcakes

2 dozen

They're gonna keep coming back for more, and more, and more of these cupcakes. That's because of the rich, chocolate surprise in the center of every one!

1 package (8 ounces) cream cheese, softened
1/3 cup sugar
1 egg
1 cup (6 ounces) semisweet chocolate chips, divided
1 package (18.25 ounces) yellow cake mix, mixed according to the package directions

Preheat the oven to 350°F. Line 24 muffin cups with paper baking cups. In a large bowl, with an electric beater on medium speed, beat the cream cheese, sugar, and egg until creamy. Place 1/4 cup chocolate chips in a microwave-safe bowl and microwave on high power for about 30 seconds, or until melted; stir until smooth. Beat the melted chips into the cream cheese mixture. With a spoon, stir in the remaining chocolate chips and set aside. Fill the baking cups two-thirds full with the cake batter. Drop a heaping teaspoon of the cream cheese mixture into the center of the batter in each cup. Bake for 15 to 20 minutes, or until a wooden toothpick inserted in the cake part comes out clean.

NOTE: Eat these just as they are, or, for extra creamy flavor, top the cupcakes with Chocolate Cream Cheese Frosting (page 173).

Chocolate Snowballs

2 dozen

I grew up enjoying a store-bought version of these, but now we can make them right in our own kitchens—for about half as much money. And don't worry—the only place these will melt is in your mouth.

1 box (18.25 ounces) chocolate cake mix, mixed according to the package directions
1 can (16 ounces) ready-to-spread white frosting
4 cups shredded coconut

Preheat the oven to 350°F. Fill 24 muffin cups that have been coated with nonstick baking spray about half-full with the cake batter. (You do not need muffin cup liners.) Bake for 14 to 16 minutes, or until a wooden toothpick inserted in the center comes out clean. Let the cupcakes cool for 10 minutes, then remove from the baking tins and place on cooling racks. Let cool completely, then freeze the cupcakes for 2 hours, until firm. Remove from the freezer and frost the top and sides of each cupcake with the frosting. Sprinkle generously with the shredded coconut, completely covering the frosting. Serve immediately or cover and let sit at room temperature until ready to serve.

NOTE: These cupcakes can be made in advance and kept frozen in an airtight container until they're needed. Then just frost, top with the coconut, and let sit at room temperature for 20 minutes before serving.

Ice Cream Muffins

1 dozen

This is something I first tried when I ran out of milk for a muffin recipe. I thought, "Hey, why not try ice cream instead?" It worked! Now I don't care if I've run out of milk when I want to make muffins.

2 cups chocolate ice cream
1 cup (6 ounces) semisweet chocolate chips
2 cups self-rising flour
2 teaspoons vanilla extract

Preheat the oven to 400°F. In a large bowl, stir the ice cream until very soft but not melted. Stir in the remaining ingredients until well blended; the mixture will be stiff. Place 12 paper baking cups in a muffin tin and fill each cup about two-thirds full with batter. Bake for 18 to 20 minutes, until a wooden toothpick inserted in the center comes out clean. Cool for about 5 minutes before removing from muffin tins.

NOTE: You can really experiment with these by using different ice cream flavors, even ones, like chocolate chip, that have chocolate or candy bits in them.

Strawberry Roll-up

10 to 12 servings

When you serve this cake roll, your friends and family will want to roll out the red carpet—for you, of course, because you've made another winner!

$\frac{3}{4}$ cup all-purpose flour
$\frac{1}{4}$ cup unsweetened cocoa
1 teaspoon baking powder
$\frac{1}{4}$ teaspoon salt
3 eggs
1 cup granulated sugar
$\frac{1}{3}$ cup water
1 teaspoon vanilla extract
Confectioners' sugar for sprinkling
$\frac{1}{2}$ cup strawberry preserves
$\frac{1}{2}$ pint (1 cup) heavy cream, whipped

Preheat the oven to 375°F. Line a 10" × 15" rimmed cookie sheet or jelly-roll pan, including the sides, with aluminum foil. Coat the foil with nonstick baking spray. In a small bowl, combine the flour, cocoa, baking powder, and salt; set aside. In a large bowl, with an electric beater on high speed, beat the eggs for 3 to 5 minutes, until soft peaks form. Gradually beat in the granulated sugar, then the water and vanilla until well blended. Reduce the speed to low and beat in the flour mixture just until smooth. Pour into the pan and bake for 10 to 12 minutes, or until a wooden toothpick inserted in the center comes out clean. Sprinkle a clean kitchen towel with confectioners' sugar and invert the cake onto the towel; peel off the aluminum foil. While it is still hot, roll the cake and the towel up from a narrow end, jelly-roll fashion, and cool on a wire rack. When cooled, unroll the cake, removing the towel. In a small bowl, fold the preserves into the whipped cream. Spread the whipped cream mixture over the top of the cake and roll it up again. Chill for at least 2 hours. When ready to use, sprinkle with confectioners' sugar, slice, and serve.

NOTE: Serve slices of this on a pool of strawberry sauce (pages 161 and 162) and garnish with fresh strawberries.

Easy as Pie

Comfort is the key with these easy versions of home-style pies!

My Own Chocolate Pie Crust

One 9-inch deep-dish pie crust

There sure are some super premade pie crusts available today that are ready for us to fill. I love to use them when I'm in a hurry, but once in a while I like to make my own chocolate crust. Why not, when it's as simple as this?!

1½ cups all-purpose flour
3 tablespoons sugar
2 tablespoons unsweetened cocoa
1 teaspoon salt
½ cup vegetable oil
2 tablespoons cold milk

If planning to use this as a prebaked shell, preheat the oven to 425°F. Sift the flour, sugar, cocoa, and salt into a 9-inch deep-dish pie plate. In a small bowl, whisk together the oil and milk, and pour over the flour mixture. Using a fork, mix until the dry ingredients are completely moist. Using your fingers, press the dough evenly over the bottom and up the sides of the plate, partly covering the rim. To use as a baked shell, prick the dough all over with a fork and bake for 12 to 15 minutes, until set, then cool and fill as desired. To use as an unbaked shell, fill with the desired filling and bake according to the pie filling directions.

Cookie Pie Crust

One 9-inch pie crust

When you use this chocolate cookie crust, you'll be giving your pies a whole new taste and texture. And there's a bonus: It's a great way to use up all those broken cookies in the bottom of the bag!

18 to 20 cream-filled chocolate sandwich cookies, finely crushed (about 2 cups)
$1/4$ cup ($1/2$ stick) butter, melted

Preheat the oven to 350°F. In a medium-sized bowl, combine the cookie crumbs and butter; mix well. Coat a 9-inch pie plate with nonstick baking spray and press the crumb mixture into the bottom and up the sides of the pan. Bake for 8 to 9 minutes, or until the crust is set. Cool and fill as desired.

NOTE: The quickest and easiest way to crush the cookies is to place them in a resealable plastic storage bag, seal tightly, and crush with a kitchen mallet or a rolling pin.

Black Forest Pie

8 to 16 servings

I bet you'll want to hide out in the forest when you're eating this pie. Why? Because you probably won't want to share it with anyone, especially not the big bad wolf!

1 package (8 ounces) cream cheese, softened
½ cup unsweetened cocoa
1 cup confectioners' sugar
1 teaspoon vanilla extract
1 container (8 ounces) frozen whipped topping, thawed
Two 9-inch chocolate graham cracker pie crusts
1 can (21 ounces) cherry pie filling

In a large bowl, with an electric beater on medium speed, beat the cream cheese and cocoa together until creamy. Slowly add the confectioners' sugar and continue beating until well blended. With a spoon, stir in the vanilla, then fold in the whipped topping. Pour the mixture into the pie crusts and chill for about 2 hours, or until firm. Top with the cherry pie filling and serve immediately, or cover and chill until ready to use.

Chocolate Eggnog Pie

6 to 8 servings

Here's something different! Sure, we're all used to having eggnog at holiday time, but this way we can give it a new twist . . . a *chocolate* twist!

1 box (4-serving size) instant chocolate pudding and pie filling
$1\frac{1}{3}$ cups prepared eggnog
1 container (8 ounces) frozen whipped topping, thawed
1 cup (6 ounces) semisweet chocolate chips, finely chopped, divided
One 9-inch chocolate graham cracker pie crust

In a medium-sized bowl, whisk together the pudding mix and eggnog for 1 to 2 minutes, or until the mixture is well blended. Fold in the whipped topping. Add $\frac{3}{4}$ cup of the chocolate chips, stirring until well blended. Spoon the filling into the pie crust and top with the remaining chocolate chips. Cover and chill for 2 hours, or until the filling is firm.

NOTE: Don't worry about having to chop the chocolate chips. Sure, you can do it by hand, but it's a lot easier if you give them a whirl in a food processor that has been fitted with its steel cutting blade. And here's a tip: The colder the chips, the easier they are to chop.

Irresistible Mocha Pie

6 to 8 servings

Once your company gets a look at this, you won't even have to ask them if they want some. They'll all be oohing and aahing because it looks (and tastes) irresistible!

1/3 cup water
1 envelope (0.25 ounce) unflavored gelatin
1 pint (2 cups) heavy cream
1/3 cup sugar
1/3 cup unsweetened cocoa
1/3 cup coffee-flavored liqueur or strong black coffee
One 9-inch chocolate graham cracker pie crust

In a small saucepan, heat the water and gelatin over medium heat, stirring constantly, for 1 to 2 minutes, until the gelatin is dissolved. Remove from the heat and allow to cool. In a large bowl, with an electric beater on high speed, beat the cream until foamy. Slowly add the sugar and cocoa and beat until the mixture is stiff. Fold in the liqueur and the cooled gelatin mixture until well blended. Spoon the mixture into the pie crust. Refrigerate for 2 hours, or until the filling is firm.

NOTE: Want to go all out? Make this in My Own Chocolate Pie Crust (page 97). Either way, you'll drive your company wild!

Turtle Pie

8 to 10 servings

You know those yummy chocolate-caramel candies that are shaped like turtles? I've put that same gooey, rich taste into this pie!

1 box (21 to 23 ounces) brownie mix
¾ cup chopped pecans, divided
One 9-inch frozen ready-to-bake deep dish pie shell, thawed
⅓ cup caramel topping

Preheat the oven to 350°F. In a large bowl, prepare the brownie mix according to the package directions. Stir in ½ cup of the pecans and pour into the pie crust. Bake for 60 to 65 minutes, or until a wooden toothpick inserted in the center comes out clean. Let cool for 20 minutes. Drizzle the caramel topping over the brownies and sprinkle with the remaining pecans.

NOTE: Be sure to have ice-cold milk on hand when you serve this!

Chocolate Silk Pie

8 servings

When you're talking about fabric, silk has always been considered among the finest and most elegant. When you're talking about pie . . . well, try this one and see if you see any similarity.

1 package (4-serving size) instant vanilla pudding and pie filling
1 package (4-serving size) instant chocolate pudding and pie filling
1/4 teaspoon ground nutmeg
1/4 teaspoon ground cinnamon
1 cup cold milk
2 cups vanilla ice cream, softened
One 9-inch graham cracker pie crust

Place all the ingredients except the crust in a large bowl; with an electric beater on medium speed, mix for about 1 minute, or until the mixture is smooth. Pour the mixture into the pie crust, cover, and freeze for at least 2 hours, or until firm. Remove from the freezer about 15 minutes before serving.

NOTE: For a nice touch, garnish this with whipped cream or whipped topping and a crushed chocolate candy bar or chocolate cookie crumbs. Cover and store any leftover pie in the freezer.

Chocolate Pecan Pie

8 servings

Pecan pie is so special that at first I was afraid to change it. I wasn't sure if I'd be able to improve upon something that's almost perfect. Boy, am I glad I tried, 'cause this Chocolate Pecan Pie is a sure winner!

1 cup light corn syrup
1 cup firmly packed light brown sugar
3 eggs
1 teaspoon vanilla extract
1½ cups coarsely chopped pecans
¾ cup (4 ½ ounces) chocolate chips
¼ cup (½ stick) butter, melted
One 9-inch frozen ready-to-bake pie shell, thawed

Preheat the oven to 350°F. In a large bowl, combine the corn syrup, brown sugar, eggs, and vanilla; stir with a spoon until thoroughly mixed. Add the pecans, chocolate chips, and butter; mix well. Pour into the pie shell and bake for 55 to 60 minutes, or until firm.

NOTE: The filling in the center will sink a bit as it cools. Oh, did you know you can buy pecans already broken into pieces? Look for them!

Chocolate Cream Pie

6 to 8 servings

I've heard that chocolate cream pie is one of the favorite pies in this country, next to apple and pumpkin. It might become the #1 favorite when this recipe gets around!

One 9-inch frozen ready-to-bake deep-dish pie shell
1 package (4-serving size) instant chocolate pudding and pie filling
1¾ cups cold milk
1 envelope (0.25 ounce) unflavored gelatin
3 tablespoons hot water
½ pint (1 cup) heavy cream
2 tablespoons sugar

Bake the pie shell according to the package directions; let cool. In a medium-sized bowl, combine the pudding mix and milk; mix well. In a small bowl, combine the gelatin and water and beat with a fork until completely dissolved. Add to the pudding mixture; mix well. Pour into the pie shell and refrigerate for 2 hours, or until the pie is set. In a medium-sized bowl, with an electric beater on medium speed, beat the cream and sugar for 2 to 4 minutes, until stiff peaks form. Spread the whipped cream over the firm pie. Serve immediately, or cover and chill until ready to serve.

NOTE: Heavy cream whips up best if you use a chilled bowl with chilled beaters. So if you can, put the bowl and beaters in the refrigerator for about a half-hour before whipping.

Traditional Boston Cream Pie

8 to 10 servings

Boston is so rich in history . . . for example, it's famous for the Boston Tea Party, the Boston Marathon, and the Battle of Bunker Hill. But did you know that Boston is also rich in taste?!

1 box (18.5 ounces) yellow cake mix
1 box (4-serving size) instant vanilla pudding and pie filling
1 cup cold milk
Chocolate Glaze (page 174)

Prepare the cake mix and bake according to the package directions for two 8-inch layers; let cool. Reserve 1 cake layer for later use (see Note). Slice the remaining cake layer in half horizontally and place the bottom half cut side up on a serving plate. In a medium-sized bowl, whisk the pudding mix and milk together until the pudding is thick and smooth; spread the pudding over the bottom cake layer. Place the other half of the cake layer cut side down over the pudding. Refrigerate while preparing the Chocolate Glaze. Allow the glaze to cool slightly before spreading it over the top of the cake. Refrigerate the glazed cake for at least 1 hour, or until the filling and glaze are set, before serving.

NOTE: I hope you're not confused by this being called a pie. Traditional Boston Cream Pie really isn't a traditional pie with a crust; it's a round layer cake with a custard filling. And because this one starts with cake mix, you're going to have a second cake layer that you don't need this time. So, you can either make two "pies" now or freeze the second cake layer for another "pie." This is so creamy good that I bet you'll use it soon!

Mocha Mousse Tarts

6 servings

I know that every once in a while you look for a new answer to "What can I serve my company for dessert?" Here it is!

4 ounces cream cheese, softened
2 teaspoons instant coffee granules
1 tablespoon warm water
¾ cup sugar
¼ cup unsweetened cocoa
½ pint (1 cup) heavy cream
6 single-serving graham cracker tart shells

In a medium-sized bowl, with an electric beater on medium speed, beat the cream cheese until smooth. In a small bowl or cup, dissolve the coffee in the water; add to the cream cheese along with the sugar and cocoa. Beat until well blended; set aside. In another medium-sized bowl, with an electric beater on high speed, beat the cream until stiff peaks form. With a spoon, gently fold the whipped cream into the cream cheese mixture, then spoon into the tart shells. Chill for at least 1 hour before serving.

NOTE: For some added pizzazz, garnish each tart with a dollop of whipped cream, some chocolate chips, or even some chocolate coffee bean candies.

Cookie Jar Favorites

Everybody's got a favorite cookie, and I'll bet you'll find yours (or a new one) here. There's always room for a cookie . . . or two!

Devilish Minty Cookies

3 to 4 dozen

Starting with cake mix means these will be a snap. Adding mint candies means they'll wake up your taste buds. One bite means you're gonna have a devilish grin on your face!

1 package (18.5 ounces) devil's food cake mix
1/3 cup vegetable oil
2 eggs
3/4 cup coarsely chopped chocolate-covered thin mint candies

Preheat the oven to 350°F. In a large bowl, combine the cake mix, oil, and eggs and beat with an electric beater for 3 to 4 minutes, until well blended. With a spoon, stir in the chopped thin mints. Drop by teaspoonfuls 2 inches apart onto cookie sheets that have been coated with nonstick baking spray. Bake for 9 to 11 minutes, or until the cookies are firm. Remove the cookies to a wire rack to cool completely.

Chocolate Macadamia Cookies

4 to 5 dozen

By simply adding a few macadamia nuts to this chocolate cookie dough, we turn ordinary into *extra*-ordinary.

2 cups all-purpose flour
$\frac{3}{4}$ cup unsweetened cocoa
1 teaspoon baking soda
$\frac{1}{2}$ teaspoon salt
$1\frac{1}{4}$ cups ($2\frac{1}{2}$ sticks) butter, softened
2 cups sugar
2 eggs
2 teaspoons vanilla extract
1 jar (7 ounces) macadamia nuts (about $1\frac{1}{2}$ cups)

Preheat the oven to 350°F. In a medium-sized bowl, combine the flour, cocoa, baking soda, and salt. In a large bowl, with an electric beater, beat the butter and sugar until light and fluffy. Add the eggs and vanilla and continue beating until creamy. Gradually add the flour mixture, beating well. Stir in the macadamia nuts. Drop by rounded teaspoonfuls 2 inches apart onto ungreased cookie sheets and bake for 8 to 10 minutes, until the cookies are firm. Cool slightly, then remove the cookies to a wire rack to cool completely.

Chocolate Pinwheels

about 4 dozen

When I was deciding what cookies to include here, I decided to try a favorite old-time cookie called Elephant Ears—but with a chocolate twist. I'm sure glad I did!

1 package (17.25 ounces) frozen puff pastry sheets, slightly thawed
¼ cup sugar
1 tablespoon unsweetened cocoa
1 egg, beaten

Preheat the oven to 400°F. On a lightly floured surface, use a rolling pin to roll out each pastry sheet to a 12-inch square. In a small bowl, combine the sugar and cocoa. Brush the pastry sheets with the beaten egg and sprinkle 2 tablespoons of the chocolate mixture evenly over each pastry sheet. Tightly roll each pastry sheet into a log and cut into ½-inch slices. Place 2 inches apart on cookie sheets that have been lightly coated with nonstick baking spray. Bake for 12 to 14 minutes, or until golden. Let cool for 2 to 3 minutes, then loosen with a spatula. Allow to cool completely on cookie sheets.

NOTE: Make sure to thaw the pastry just until slightly thawed. Otherwise, it'll be too hard to handle.

Chocolate Biscotti

about 4 dozen

In Italian, *biscotti* refers to a twice-baked cookie. And when you taste these, you'll know it must also mean twice as *buono* (good)!

2½ cups all-purpose flour
¾ cup unsweetened cocoa
2 cups sugar
½ teaspoon salt
1 teaspoon baking soda
5 eggs
1 teaspoon vanilla extract
1 cup (5 ounces) whole blanched almonds

Preheat the oven to 350°F. In a large bowl, combine all the ingredients except the almonds; mix well with a spoon. Stir in the almonds until well blended; the dough will be thick and sticky. Place half of the dough on a 10″× 15″ rimmed cookie sheet that has been coated with nonstick baking spray; form a slightly rounded 4″× 12″ loaf that is about ¾ inch thick. Repeat with the remaining dough, place next to first loaf, and bake for 30 minutes. Remove from the oven and reduce the temperature to 325°F. Allow the loaves to cool for 20 to 25 minutes, then cut into ½-inch-thick slices. Lay the slices cut side down on a cookie sheet and bake for 15 more minutes. Turn the cookies over and bake for another 15 minutes or until very crisp. Allow to cool, then store in an airtight container.

NOTE: Biscotti are very crunchy. That's why they're perfect for dunking in coffee, tea, hot chocolate, cappuccino, and espresso.

Peanut Butter Wraparounds

2 to 2½ dozen

Just wrap these chocolates in peanut butter, and watch everybody go "nuts." (Maybe you'd better make a double batch!)

1 cup sugar
1 cup creamy peanut butter
1 egg
1 teaspoon vanilla extract
24 to 30 chocolate candy kisses

Preheat the oven to 325°F. In a medium-sized bowl, combine the sugar, peanut butter, egg, and vanilla; mix well. Wrap a heaping teaspoon of dough completely around each piece of chocolate. Bake on ungreased cookie sheets for 13 to 15 minutes, or until the cookies are light golden. Let cool before removing from the cookie sheet.

NOTE: For an extra added surprise, you could use almond or white chocolate candy kisses.

Zucchini Cookies

about 4 dozen

Zucchini cookies in a chocolate book? You've got it—a chocolate cookie that's got good-for-you zucchini. And the kids never have to know that there are veggies in them.

½ cup (1 stick) butter, softened
1 cup sugar
1 egg, beaten
2 cups all-purpose flour
1 teaspoon baking soda
1 teaspoon ground cinnamon
½ teaspoon salt
1 cup grated zucchini (about 1 small zucchini)
1 cup raisins
1 cup chopped walnuts
1 cup (6 ounces) semisweet chocolate chips

Preheat the oven to 350°F. In a large bowl, cream together the butter and sugar until light and fluffy. Gradually add the egg, flour, baking soda, cinnamon, and salt; mix well. Stir in the zucchini, raisins, walnuts, and chocolate chips. Drop by teaspoonfuls 2 inches apart onto cookie sheets that have been coated with nonstick baking spray. Bake for 15 to 20 minutes, or until golden. Do not overbake. Allow to cool for 2 to 3 minutes, then remove to wire racks to cool completely.

Meringue Coconut Macaroons

about 2 dozen

These remind me of a cookie I first had at a contest I judged, but with these I figured out how to cut the work in half and still have that winning taste.

2 egg whites
½ teaspoon vanilla extract
⅔ cup sugar
1½ teaspoons unsweetened cocoa
1 cup shredded coconut

Preheat the oven to 325°F. In a medium-sized bowl, beat the egg whites and vanilla with an electric beater until soft peaks form. Gradually add the sugar and cocoa and beat until stiff peaks form. Fold in the shredded coconut. Drop by teaspoonfuls onto a cookie sheet that has been coated with nonstick baking spray. Bake for 18 to 20 minutes, until puffy and firm. Allow to cool for 2 to 3 minutes, then remove to wire racks to cool completely. Store in an airtight container.

Ultimate Chocolate Chunk Cookies

3 to 4 dozen cookies

The name says it all: Ultimate, yes. Chocolate, yes. Chunky, yes. See, now you know where the name comes from.

2 cups all-purpose flour
1 teaspoon baking soda
½ teaspoon salt
½ cup (1 stick) butter, softened
½ cup vegetable shortening
½ cup granulated sugar
¾ cup firmly packed light brown sugar
1 teaspoon vanilla extract
1 egg
2 cups (12 ounces) semisweet chocolate chunks
½ cup chopped nuts (optional)

Preheat the oven to 375°F. In a medium-sized bowl, combine the flour, baking soda, and salt; set aside. In a large bowl, combine the butter, shortening, sugars, and vanilla; beat until creamy. Beat in the egg, then gradually add the flour mixture, mixing well. Stir in the chocolate chunks and nuts with a wooden spoon; mix well. Drop by rounded teaspoonfuls 2 inches apart onto ungreased cookie sheets. Bake for 8 to 10 minutes, until the edges are golden. Cool on cookie sheets for 2 minutes, then remove the cookies to a wire rack to cool completely.

White-Freckled Cookies

about 2 dozen

After I decide to make these, I'm left with one tough decision to tackle: Which part do I like better—the white chocolate chips or the chocolate cookie dough? Now that's a yummy task!

1¾ cups all-purpose flour
¼ teaspoon baking soda
1 cup (2 sticks) butter, softened
1 cup granulated sugar
½ cup firmly packed light brown sugar
1 teaspoon vanilla extract
⅓ cup unsweetened cocoa
2 tablespoons light cream
2 cups (12 ounces) white baking chips

Preheat the oven to 350°F. In a large bowl, combine the flour and baking soda; set aside. In another large bowl, with an electric beater, cream together the butter and sugars; add the vanilla and mix well. Add the cocoa and beat until well blended. Add the cream, then, beating on low speed, gradually add the flour mixture; beat until mixed. With a spoon, stir in the baking chips. Drop by heaping tablespoonfuls onto greased cookie sheets; flatten the cookies slightly with the palm of your hand. Bake for 12 to 14 minutes, until golden around the edges; the cookies should still feel soft. Do not overbake. Cool for 2 minutes on the cookie sheets, then remove to wire racks to cool completely.

Chocolate-Covered-Raisin Cookies

about 4 dozen

I'm a true believer in the saying that everything happens for a reason. Recently, when I was about to add the raisins to a favorite cookie recipe, I discovered that we were out of raisins—but I realized that we *did* have some chocolate-covered raisins. Can you guess what I did? Yup, I used those instead . . . and was my family glad I did!

1 cup (2 sticks) butter, softened
¾ cup granulated sugar
⅓ cup firmly packed light brown sugar
2 eggs
2 teaspoons vanilla extract
2¼ cups all-purpose flour
½ teaspoon baking powder
2 cups (about 14 ounces) chocolate-covered raisins

Preheat the oven to 300°F. In a large bowl, combine the butter and sugars. Beat with an electric beater until fluffy. Add the eggs and vanilla and continue to beat until creamy. Gradually add the flour and baking powder, mixing until well combined. With a spoon, stir in the chocolate-covered raisins. Drop by heaping tablespoonfuls 2 inches apart onto ungreased baking sheets. Bake for 18 to 20 minutes, or until the edges are golden. Transfer the cookies immediately to a cool flat surface to cool completely.

Twisted Chocolate Pretzel Cookies

about 32

Put on your thinking cap to come up with all sorts of ways to shape these "pretzels." Be traditional or wild . . . the great taste will shine through any shape.

1⅔ cups all-purpose flour
¼ cup unsweetened cocoa
¾ cup (1½ sticks) butter, softened
½ cup granulated sugar
¼ cup firmly packed brown sugar
1 egg, separated
3 tablespoons milk
1 teaspoon vanilla extract
6 to 7 sugar cubes, coarsely crushed

Preheat the oven to 350°F. In a small bowl, combine the flour and cocoa and set aside. In a large bowl, beat together the butter, sugars, egg yolk, milk, and vanilla until blended. Gradually blend in the flour mixture until smooth. Cover the bowl with plastic wrap and chill for 1 hour. Divide the chilled dough into 4 equal pieces and divide each quarter into 8 equal pieces. Roll each piece on a lightly floured board with the palm of your hand into a rope approximately 8 inches long. Twist each into a pretzel (or other desired) shape. Place 1 inch apart on a cookie sheet that has been coated with nonstick baking spray. Lightly beat the egg white and brush it over the "pretzels"; sprinkle with the crushed sugar cubes. Bake for 12 to 14 minutes, until the cookies are firm when lightly touched. Let cool slightly, then remove to a wire rack.

Crispy Crunchies

3 to 4 dozen

If you're like me, you still get a kick out of your breakfast cereal making those popping noises. And when you crunch on that cereal mixed into your chocolate cookies, you'll get the noise teamed with great chocolate taste (and a lot of disappearing cookies).

½ cup granulated sugar
½ cup firmly packed light brown sugar
¾ cup (1½ sticks) butter, softened
1 egg
2 teaspoons vanilla extract
2 cups all-purpose flour
¼ cup unsweetened cocoa
½ teaspoon baking soda
¼ teaspoon salt
2 crisped-rice chocolate candy bars (5 ounces each), coarsely chopped
1 cup crispy rice cereal

Preheat the oven to 300°F. In a large bowl, with an electric beater on medium speed, beat the sugars and butter until well blended. Add the egg and vanilla and continue to beat until light and fluffy. Add the flour, cocoa, baking soda, and salt and blend well. With a spoon, stir in the candy bar chunks and cereal just until combined. Drop by rounded tablespoonfuls about 2 inches apart onto ungreased cookie sheets. Bake for 16 to 18 minutes, or until the edges are browned. Remove the cookies to a wire rack to cool completely.

Chocolate Blossoms

about 2 dozen

Sure, flowers blossom from the heat of the sun, and in no time these cookies will be blossoming from the heat of your oven.

½ cup unsweetened cocoa
¼ cup (½ stick) butter, melted
1 cup all-purpose flour, divided
1 cup granulated sugar
2 eggs
1 teaspoon almond extract
1 teaspoon baking soda
¼ teaspoon salt
¼ cup chopped almonds
¼ cup confectioners' sugar

In a large bowl, stir the cocoa into the melted butter. Cool slightly, then stir in ½ cup flour, the granulated sugar, eggs, almond extract, baking soda, and salt. Beat until well blended. Stir in the remaining ½ cup flour and the almonds until blended. Cover and chill the dough until firm, at least 3 hours, or overnight. Preheat the oven to 300°F. Shape the dough into 1-inch balls and roll each ball in the confectioners' sugar. Place the balls 3 inches apart on a cookie sheet that has been coated with nonstick baking spray. Bake for 10 to 12 minutes, or until firm when lightly touched and the tops have "blossomed" (cracked). Immediately remove from the cookie sheets and cool completely on a wire rack.

NOTE: I recommend placing the confectioners' sugar in a shallow pie plate and rolling each cookie in it to completely cover it.

Blond Macadamia Nut Cookies

about 5 dozen

If you tell the kids they can have these as an after-school treat, watch for them to come running right home—along with lots of friends!

2⅓ cups all-purpose flour
1 teaspoon baking soda
1 teaspoon salt
1 cup (2 sticks) butter
¾ cup firmly packed light brown sugar
¾ cup granulated sugar
2 eggs
1 teaspoon vanilla extract
2 cups (12 ounces) white baking chips
1 jar (7 ounces) macadamia nuts (about 1½ cups)

Preheat the oven to 350°F. In a medium-sized bowl, mix together the flour, baking soda, and salt; set aside. In a large bowl, with an electric beater, cream the butter and sugars together until creamy. Add the eggs and vanilla and continue beating until fluffy. Gradually add the flour mixture, mixing well. With a spoon, stir in the baking chips and nuts. Drop the dough by heaping teaspoonfuls onto ungreased cookie sheets and bake for 9 to 12 minutes, or until golden. Remove the cookies to a wire rack to cool.

NOTE: If you want to coarsely chop the macadamia nuts, go ahead. I like to use them whole so that I can get a big nutty crunch in every bite.

Chocolate Shortbread Cookies

2½ to 3 dozen

Sometimes you feel like a simple cookie without any fancy add-ins or decorations. Bingo!

1 cup (2 sticks) butter, softened
¾ cup sugar
1¾ cups all-purpose flour
½ cup unsweetened cocoa

Preheat the oven to 300°F. In a large bowl, with an electric beater, beat the butter and sugar until creamy. Add the flour and cocoa and continue beating until the dough holds together. Form the dough into 1½-inch balls and place 3 inches apart on a cookie sheet that has been lightly coated with nonstick baking spray. Press the balls flat with the palm of your hand and bake for 30 to 35 minutes, or until the edges of the cookies are firm. Allow to cool for 2 to 3 minutes, then remove to wire racks to cool completely.

Chocolate Haystacks

2 to 3 dozen

When you make these, you'll see where they got their name—because they look like miniature haystacks! I bet you never thought you'd be putting chow mein noodles into cookies, huh?

1 cup (6 ounces) semisweet chocolate chips
1 cup (6 ounces) peanut butter chips
1 tablespoon vegetable shortening
1 package (6 ounces) chow mein noodles, coarsely broken

Place the chocolate and peanut butter chips and the vegetable shortening in a medium-sized microwave-safe bowl. Heat in the microwave on high power for 1 minute, then stir the mixture. Continue to heat for 15-second intervals, stirring frequently, until the chips are melted and the mixture is smooth. With a spoon, stir in the chow mein noodles until well combined. Drop by teaspoonfuls onto a waxed paper–lined cookie sheet. Chill for about 1 hour, or until firm.

Soft Chocolate Marshmallow Sandwiches

about 20 sandwiches

Oh, yeah! With chocolate and marshmallow, you just can't miss. And believe me, this is one sandwich cookie you don't want to miss!

2 cups all-purpose flour
$1\frac{1}{2}$ teaspoons baking soda
$\frac{1}{2}$ teaspoon salt
$\frac{1}{2}$ cup vegetable shortening
$\frac{1}{2}$ cup granulated sugar
1 egg
$\frac{1}{2}$ cup unsweetened cocoa
1 cup milk
1 teaspoon vanilla extract

Filling:
$\frac{3}{4}$ cup ($1\frac{1}{2}$ sticks) butter, softened
$1\frac{1}{3}$ cups confectioners' sugar
1 cup marshmallow creme (about $\frac{1}{2}$ of a $7\frac{1}{2}$-ounce jar)
$\frac{1}{2}$ teaspoon vanilla extract

Preheat the oven to 400°F. In a large bowl, combine the flour, baking soda, and salt. In another large bowl, with an electric beater, beat the shortening, granulated sugar, and egg until creamy. Beat in the cocoa. Beat into the flour mixture alternately with the milk and 1 teaspoon vanilla. Drop by teaspoonfuls onto ungreased cookie sheets. Flatten the dough lightly to get a wider, thinner cookie, because they rise while baking. Bake for 8 to 10 minutes. While the cookies are baking, combine the filling ingredients in a medium-sized bowl and beat until smooth and creamy. Remove the cookies to wire racks. Frost the flat side of half of the cookies with the filling and put the remaining cookies on top, making sandwiches. Chill until the filling is firm, then serve; store leftovers in the refrigerator.

The Chocolate "Bar"

Isn't it time to relax and enjoy a creamy, smooth milk shake, frothy egg cream, or soothing hot cocoa?!

Hot Chocolate Mix

3¾ cups mix, about 15 servings

Have you ever had a craving for a mug of hot cocoa, only to find that you were out of those individual little envelopes of packaged hot chocolate mix? Now you can make your own cocoa mix so that you'll never have to worry about running out again.

2 cups nonfat dry milk
¾ cup sugar
½ cup unsweetened cocoa
½ cup dry nondairy creamer
⅛ teaspoon salt

In a large bowl, combine all the ingredients; mix well. Store in an airtight container. To make a mug of hot chocolate, simply place ¼ cup of the mix in a mug and add ¾ cup boiling water; stir to blend.

Chilled Hot Chocolate

4 to 5 servings

We've all heard the expression "If you can't take the heat, get out of the kitchen." No, don't do that! Don't leave the kitchen! Instead, make this chilled cocoa.

4 envelopes (1 ounce each) instant hot cocoa mix (½ cup total)
1½ cups warm water
1½ cups half-and-half
2 scoops vanilla ice cream

In a blender, dissolve the hot cocoa mix in the warm water. Add the half-and-half and ice cream and blend on high speed until smooth and creamy. Serve immediately.

NOTE: Even though this is served cold, you can still top each serving with a few miniature marshmallows if you'd like.

Cocoa Peppermint Frosty

4 servings

The fresh taste of peppermint in a chocolatey milk shake sure makes your taste buds and tummy feel good.

6 red-and-white peppermint hard candies, unwrapped
2 tablespoons sugar
2 tablespoons unsweetened cocoa
2 cups milk, divided
1 large scoop vanilla ice cream

Place the candies in a blender, cover, and blend until finely crushed. **Be sure that all of the candy is finely crushed.** Add the sugar, cocoa, and 1 cup milk; blend well. Add the remaining milk and the ice cream. Blend until smooth and creamy. Serve immediately.

NOTE: If you want to enjoy this with a bit less fat, you can use skim milk and low-fat frozen yogurt or low-fat ice cream and it will still be a smooth and creamy treat.

Mochachino

8 servings

Are you looking for a hot drink that's a pleasant change from plain coffee? If you simply add a little chocolate syrup, your friends will wonder where you got the fancy flavored coffee.

6 measuring cups brewed coffee
½ cup chocolate-flavored syrup
½ cup Whipped Cream (page 176) or frozen whipped topping, thawed

Pour the hot brewed coffee into a medium-sized saucepan and add the chocolate syrup; stir well. Pour into individual cups and top each with a dollop of whipped cream.

NOTE: You can use a freshly brewed pot of coffee or instant coffee. Make it however it's easiest for you.

New York Egg Cream

5 to 6 servings

Times Square, Chinatown, Harlem, and Little Italy—all important parts of New York City. And we can't forget the Lower East Side, the home of the best New York egg creams. Try one today . . . without a plane ticket!

3/4 cup chocolate-flavored syrup
2 bottles (10 ounces each) cold club soda or seltzer water
1 1/2 cups cold milk

Pour the chocolate-flavored syrup into a pitcher, then add the club soda and stir just until mixed. Add the milk and stir just to combine. Immediately pour into tall glasses and serve ice-cold.

NOTE: Make sure that the club soda (or seltzer) has plenty of carbonation, then drink up . . . with a straw, of course! You're going to be surprised by how tasty these are . . . and they don't even contain any eggs or cream.

St. Patrick's Day Cocktails

4 to 6 servings

The Irish sure have shared an abundance of great food and drink with the rest of us. Sure, there's the obvious corned beef and cabbage, and Irish soda bread. Instead of washing those down with an Irish beer, why not try a fun chocolate alternative for a change? It's just what the leprechaun ordered.

1 can (14 ounces) sweetened condensed milk
1½ cups heavy cream
1½ tablespoons chocolate-flavored syrup
¾ cup Irish or other whiskey

Combine all of the ingredients in a blender and blend on medium speed until thoroughly mixed. Cover and refrigerate until ready to serve, then blend again on medium speed and serve over ice in cordial glasses or juice-sized glasses.

NOTE: This drink can be made ahead of time and stored, covered, in the refrigerator for up to 1 week. For a thick, rich Irish milk shake, add a scoop or two of vanilla ice cream and blend until smooth.

Extra-Thick Chocolate Shake

4 servings

Hooray! No more having to search for a home-style diner to get a real thick chocolate shake. Now you can order up one of these in your own kitchen.

3 large scoops vanilla ice cream
2 cups milk
1/4 cup chocolate-flavored syrup
1 teaspoon vanilla extract
1/4 cup Whipped Cream (page 176) or frozen whipped topping, thawed

In a blender, combine the ice cream, milk, syrup, and vanilla and blend on high speed until thoroughly mixed. Pour into 4 glasses and top each with a dollop of whipped cream. Serve immediately.

NOTE: Don't forget the straws!

Cookies 'n' Cream Shake

4 servings

After school is the right time for a snack of milk and cookies. Why not surprise the kids and serve it all in one glass?

10 cream-filled chocolate sandwich cookies
3 large scoops vanilla ice cream
1½ cups milk

Place the cookies in a blender and process on high speed until finely crushed. Add the ice cream and milk and blend until thoroughly mixed. Pour into 4 glasses and serve immediately.

NOTE: This is a super way to use up about 1 cup of broken cookies from the bottom of the package.

Chocolate Mud Slide

4 servings

True, a mud slide can be a powerful thing. And I've got one here that I'll bet you won't mind experiencing again and again!

3 large scoops chocolate ice cream
1 cup milk
2 cups ice cubes
3 tablespoons coffee-flavored liqueur
3 tablespoons vodka (optional)

In a blender, combine all the ingredients and blend on medium speed until thoroughly mixed. Pour into glasses and serve.

NOTE: This dessert is for adults only. And remember, never drink and drive. When you've experienced a Chocolate Mud Slide, let someone else do the driving.

Chocolate Malted

4 servings

So, you've always wanted to know how to make a real old-fashioned chocolate malted? Here it is, in my shortcut version and better than ever.

3 large scoops vanilla ice cream
$1\frac{1}{2}$ cups milk
1 bag (7 ounces) chocolate malted milk balls, crushed (see Note)

In a blender, combine all the ingredients and blend on high speed until thoroughly mixed. Pour into tall glasses and serve immediately.

NOTE: Here's an easy way to crush the malted milk balls: Place them in a resealable plastic storage bag, close tightly, and crush with a rolling pin. You know, you can use whole milk, 2%, 1%, or skim milk—the choice is yours. And if you want to lighten it up, use low-fat frozen yogurt in place of the vanilla ice cream.

Banana Smoothie

4 to 5 servings

Looking for something to pick you up after your workout? This'll surely give you a burst of energy—and a burst of flavor—in each sip.

2 cups low-fat milk
2 medium-sized ripe bananas, peeled and sliced
⅓ cup chocolate-flavored syrup
2 large scoops vanilla frozen yogurt

In a blender, combine all the ingredients and blend on medium speed until smooth. Pour into glasses and serve.

Melt-in-Your-Mouth Treats

Making chocolate candies and other goodies has never been this easy . . . really!

Almond Marble Bark

about 1 pound

Do you know why this is so popular, besides the taste? Because we get to break up the bark into bite-sized pieces. I don't know which is more fun—breaking it up or eating it!

2 cups (12 ounces) milk chocolate chips
1 tablespoon vegetable shortening
½ cup sliced almonds, toasted (see Note)
⅓ cup (2 ounces) white baking chips

In a medium-sized microwave-safe bowl, heat the milk chocolate chips with the shortening on high power for 1 to 2 minutes, stirring often, until the chocolate is melted and the mixture is smooth. Stir in the almonds, then pour into an 8-inch square baking pan lined with aluminum foil that has been coated with nonstick baking spray. Place the white baking chips in a heavy-duty resealable plastic storage bag and heat in the microwave on high power for about 45 seconds, until melted. Knead the chips until smooth. Cut a tiny corner from the bag and drizzle the white chocolate over the chocolate in the pan. Swirl with a knife. Chill for about 1 hour, or until set. Lift the foil from the pan, then break the bark into pieces and serve.

NOTE: To toast the almonds, place them on a rimmed cookie sheet in a single layer and bake them in a preheated 350°F. oven for 3 to 5 minutes, just until golden. Watch them carefully to avoid burning.

Truffles

about 2 dozen

Why not make these an elegant addition to your holiday cookie platters, or even as a special go-along for plain vanilla ice cream. Sometimes the simplest things are the best.

½ cup evaporated milk
¼ cup sugar
2 teaspoons instant coffee granules
1 tablespoon hot water
2 cups (12 ounces) semisweet chocolate or white baking chips
½ cup finely chopped toasted almonds (see Note, page 145)

In a small heavy saucepan, combine the evaporated milk and sugar; heat over medium heat until the mixture comes to a rolling boil. Boil for 3 minutes, stirring constantly; remove from the heat. In a cup, dissolve the coffee in the hot water; add to the milk mixture along with the chocolate chips and stir until the chocolate is melted and the mixture is smooth. Cover and chill for 1 hour. Shape into 1-inch balls, then roll in the almonds. Place on a cookie sheet, cover, and chill for at least 2 hours, or until firm.

NOTE: I usually make two batches at a time—one batch of semisweet chocolate truffles and one batch of white chocolate truffles. And I like to roll them in all kinds of toppings besides toasted almonds or other chopped nuts, like colored sprinkles, colored granulated sugars, cocoa powder, and even crushed candy bars.

Special Almond Clusters

about 3 dozen

Nutty, yes. Easy, yes . . . and sinfully special.

2 cups (12 ounces) semisweet chocolate chips
1 can (14 ounces) sweetened condensed milk
2 cups coarsely chopped roasted almonds (see Note)

In a medium-sized saucepan, combine the chocolate chips and condensed milk over low heat; stir constantly until the chips are melted and the mixture is smooth. Remove from the heat and stir in the almonds; mix until the almonds are well coated. Drop by heaping teaspoonfuls onto a foil-lined cookie sheet. Cover and chill for at least 2 hours before serving. Store in the refrigerator in an airtight container.

NOTE: To roast the almonds, place them on a rimmed cookie sheet in a single layer and bake them in a preheated 350°F. oven for 5 to 8 minutes, shaking the sheet occasionally, just until the almonds are golden. Keep an eye on them to make sure that they don't burn. Allow the almonds to cool completely before using.

No-Bake Oatmeal Drops

about 4 dozen

Oatmeal is sure a big breakfast favorite. But why not enjoy the "good for you" breakfast cereal as a snack—anytime?!

½ cup (1 stick) butter
½ cup milk
2 cups sugar
3 cups rolled oats (not instant)
1 cup shredded coconut
½ cup unsweetened cocoa
1 teaspoon salt
1 teaspoon vanilla extract

In a medium-sized saucepan, heat the butter, milk, and sugar over medium heat until the butter melts. Reduce the heat to medium-low and simmer for 5 minutes, stirring occasionally. Add the remaining ingredients except the vanilla and simmer for 2 more minutes, stirring frequently. Remove from the heat, stir in the vanilla, and allow to cool slightly. Drop by heaping teaspoonfuls onto a cookie sheet that has been lined with waxed paper. Allow to cool and set. Store in an airtight container.

Meringue Kisses

about 5 dozen

Pucker up, 'cause here's the recipe for one of the sweetest kisses you'll ever have . . . chocolate meringue kisses, that is.

2 egg whites
½ teaspoon vanilla extract
¼ teaspoon cream of tartar
⅔ cup sugar
¼ cup finely crushed saltine crackers
¾ cup (4½ ounces) semisweet chocolate chips

Preheat the oven to 300°F. In a medium-sized bowl, with an electric beater on medium speed, beat the egg whites until soft peaks form. Beat in the vanilla and cream of tartar. Gradually add the sugar and continue to beat until stiff dry peaks are formed. Gently fold in the cracker crumbs and chocolate chips. Drop the meringue by heaping teaspoonfuls onto a baking sheet that has been coated with nonstick baking spray. Bake for 20 to 25 minutes, or until the meringues are golden. Turn off the oven and let the kisses sit in the oven for 30 minutes. Remove the kisses from the oven and let cool completely before storing in an airtight container.

Fast Chocolate Pecan Fudge

about 5 dozen

This brings back memories of the county fair, when I always looked forward to buying a box of homemade pecan fudge. I'm sure glad that now I can create that taste whenever I want—in minutes.

$\frac{2}{3}$ cup evaporated milk
$1\frac{2}{3}$ cups sugar
$\frac{1}{2}$ teaspoon salt
$1\frac{1}{2}$ cups miniature marshmallows or 16 large marshmallows, cut into quarters
$1\frac{1}{2}$ cups (9 ounces) semisweet chocolate chips
$\frac{1}{2}$ cup chopped pecans
1 teaspoon vanilla extract

In a medium-sized saucepan, bring the milk, sugar, and salt to a boil over medium heat. Continue boiling for 5 minutes, stirring constantly. Remove from the heat and add the marshmallows, chocolate chips, nuts, and vanilla. Stir for 1 to 2 minutes, or until the marshmallows and chocolate are melted and the mixture is creamy. Pour into an 8-inch square baking dish lined with aluminum foil that has been coated with nonstick baking spray, and let cool. Cut into 1-inch squares.

Turtle Fudge

about 4 dozen

It's kind of ironic that this is called turtle fudge since, when I think of turtles, I think of something that moves slowly. And that's *not* this recipe . . . it moves really *fast*!

2½ cups sugar
½ cup (1 stick) butter
⅔ cup evaporated milk
2 cups miniature marshmallows
2 cups (12 ounces) semisweet chocolate chips
1 cup chopped walnuts
2 teaspoons vanilla extract
24 caramel candies, quartered

Line a 9" × 13" baking dish with aluminum foil so that it extends over the sides of the dish. Coat the foil with nonstick baking spray. In a large saucepan, combine the sugar, butter, and milk over medium heat. Bring to a boil, stirring constantly. Boil, continuing to stir, for 5 minutes, then remove from the heat. Add the marshmallows and chocolate chips and stir until melted. Stir in the walnuts, vanilla, and caramel candies. Pour into the foil-lined dish and allow to cool to room temperature. Cut into squares. Lift the foil from the baking dish, then remove the fudge squares. Cover and store in the refrigerator.

Chocolate Peanut Fudge

about 5 dozen

I always treat my neighbors to gift boxes of this for a little something sweet during the holidays. It must be good, 'cause my neighbors and I get along well!

2 cups (12 ounces) semisweet chocolate chips
½ cup creamy peanut butter
½ cup milk
3 cups confectioners' sugar
½ cup chopped salted peanuts

In a large saucepan over low heat or a double boiler over warm water, melt the chocolate, stirring constantly until smooth; remove from the heat. Stir in the peanut butter and milk until well mixed. Add the confectioners' sugar 1 cup at a time, mixing well after each addition; mix until smooth. Spread the mixture in an 8-inch square baking dish that has been lined with aluminum foil. Sprinkle the peanuts over the top, pushing them gently into the fudge. Cover and chill for about 1 hour, until set. Lift the foil out of the pan and remove the fudge. Place on a cutting board and cut into 1-inch squares. Cover and store in the refrigerator or in a cool, dry place.

Peanut Butter–Chocolate Candy

about 4 dozen

I can't guarantee this candy. Well, yes, it tastes good, it's easy to make, and it works every time I make it. What I can't guarantee is how long it'll last before it's all gobbled up!

1 cup creamy peanut butter
½ pound (2 sticks) butter, melted
4 cups (1 pound) confectioners' sugar
1 cup graham cracker crumbs
2 cups (12 ounces) semisweet chocolate chips

In a large bowl, combine all the ingredients except the chocolate. Spread the mixture on a 10" × 15" rimmed cookie sheet that has been coated with nonstick baking spray. In a medium-sized microwave-safe bowl, heat the chocolate chips on high power for about 1 minute, stirring often and melting at additional 10-second intervals, until the chocolate is melted and smooth. Spread evenly over the peanut butter base. Chill for 15 minutes, then cut into squares in the pan. Serve immediately, or cover and keep chilled until ready to use.

Gooey Caramel Popcorn Balls

about 2 dozen

Popcorn is more popular than ever! We eat it at the movies, at the circus, at ball games, and as a quick snack. But what about fancier occasions? How 'bout making chocolate popcorn balls?!

1 cup (6 ounces) milk chocolate chips
½ cup light corn syrup
½ cup water
1 cup sugar
⅛ teaspoon salt
2 tablespoons butter
1 teaspoon vanilla extract
3 quarts popped popcorn

In a heavy saucepan, combine the chocolate chips and corn syrup over medium heat, stirring until the chocolate melts. Stir in the water, sugar, and salt. Without stirring again, heat the mixture to boiling and cook for 35 to 40 minutes, or until the mixture reaches the soft ball stage (245°F. on a candy thermometer; see Note). Remove from the heat and add the butter and vanilla; stir until the butter melts. Put the popcorn in a large bowl and pour the chocolate mixture over the popcorn; let cool slightly. With your hands, carefully form the popcorn into 2-inch balls and place on waxed paper–lined cookie sheets. (If the mixture is too hot, let it cool a bit more before proceeding.) Allow the balls to cool completely at room temperature, then serve, or store in an airtight container until ready to use.

NOTE: To test the chocolate caramel for the soft ball stage: Drop a bit of the mixture from a teaspoon into a glass of cold water. If it forms a soft ball, then it has reached the soft ball stage. If not, continue to cook the mixture, then test it again after a bit.

Chocolate-Dipped Fruit

Just bring out some chocolate-dipped fruit and watch your gang come running. Eat up all the chocolate-dipped fruit and watch them disappear just as quickly!

2 cups (12 ounces) semisweet chocolate chips
Your favorite fresh or dried fruits (see below)

Melt (don't overheat) the chocolate chips in any of these ways:

- in a saucepan over low heat, stirring constantly.
- in the top of a double boiler (over simmering water) over low heat, stirring occasionally.
- in a stainless-steel bowl over a saucepan of simmering water.
- in the microwave in a microwave-safe container (on medium or high power for 1 to 3 minutes).

When the chocolate is melted, remove it from the heat and dip your choice of fruit into it. (To keep it neat, you can insert a skewer or fork into the fruit to dip it.) Shake any excess chocolate back into the pan and place the dipped fruit in a single layer on a waxed paper–lined cookie sheet until the chocolate firms up.

Here are some tips to help with your creations:

- Always clean and pat fruit completely dry before dipping it in the chocolate.
- Cut fruit into bite-sized pieces before dipping.
- Fruits that darken when exposed to air (bananas, apples, peaches, etc.) are best if completely coated with chocolate.
- Strawberries, apricots, and dried or candied fruits work well coated just halfway with chocolate.

- Fruit that is totally coated should be refrigerated; half-dipped fruit should be left at room temperature and used within 8 to 12 hours.

NOTE: Be careful not to allow any water to mix with the chocolate, because it will become grainy and will tighten up. If this happens, add 1 teaspoon of vegetable shortening to the chocolate and allow it to melt before continuing to dip fruit.

Special-Occasion Chocolate Cups

½ dozen

Can you guess how I came up with this name? Because I can make them in no time for family birthdays and other celebrations. I fill them with the guest of honor's favorite filling (or whatever filling I'm in the mood for).

1 cup (6 ounces) semisweet chocolate chips
1 tablespoon vegetable shortening

Place 6 paper baking cups into 6 muffin tins. In a small saucepan, heat the chocolate and shortening over low heat for 1 to 2 minutes, stirring until the chocolate melts and the mixture is smooth. Starting at the top edge of each paper cup, spoon the chocolate over the insides of the cups, completely covering the inside of each cup with about 4 teaspoons of the mixture. Refrigerate the cups until firm, about 25 to 30 minutes. Remove the paper from the chocolate and place the cups on a serving plate; chill until ready to use. Before serving, fill with your favorite pudding, mousse, or ice cream.

NOTE: I love making these 'cause I can fill them with something different every time. Sometimes I even use a variety of fillings so I can present a really colorful platter!

Sinful Sauces, Frostings, and Glazes

Use these for drizzling and topping, mixing and matching with cakes, pies, brownies, and bars . . . even cookies and candies!

Summer Strawberry Sauce

about $1\frac{1}{2}$ cups

Here's a quick-cooking strawberry sauce that has a richer body than the Strawberry Sauce on the next page. That one uses frozen strawberries and this one uses fresh, so make 'em both and have your own taste test!

2 cups sliced fresh strawberries (about 1 pint)
$1\frac{3}{4}$ cups water, divided
$\frac{1}{3}$ cup sugar
1 tablespoon cornstarch

Place the sliced strawberries in a medium-sized saucepan with $1\frac{1}{2}$ cups water and the sugar. Cook over medium heat for 25 minutes, stirring occasionally. In a small bowl, mix the remaining $\frac{1}{4}$ cup water with the cornstarch, and slowly stir into the strawberry mixture. Reduce the heat to low and simmer for 5 to 8 minutes, or until slightly thickened, stirring occasionally.

NOTE: Add 1 or 2 drops of red food color to give the sauce a ruby-red finish.

Blender Strawberry Sauce

about 2 cups

It takes two—two ingredients and two minutes—to make this anytime sauce for chocolate cake, ice cream, or whatever you want.

1 bag (16 ounces) frozen strawberries
½ cup sugar

Place the strawberries in a blender or in a food processor that has been fitted with its steel cutting blade. Blend or process for 1 to 2 minutes, or until the strawberries are puréed. Add the sugar and blend until well combined.

Raspberry Sauce

1¼ cups

There's a saying that when life gives you lemons, you should make lemonade. I agree. And to take that even further, I say that when life gives you raspberries, you've got to make Raspberry Sauce!

1 pint fresh raspberries or 1 bag (16 ounces) frozen raspberries
¼ cup sugar

In a small saucepan, combine the raspberries and sugar and cook over low heat, stirring occasionally, for about 5 minutes, or until the sugar has dissolved. Place the mixture in a blender and blend at high speed until smooth. Serve warm, or chill and serve cold.

NOTE: You may want to add more or less sugar, depending upon how sweet your raspberries are and how sweet you like your sauce. If you'd prefer a seedless sauce, press the blended sauce through a fine sieve with a wooden spoon to remove the seeds.

Vanilla Sauce

$3\frac{1}{2}$ cups

Don't you love it when you can take everyday, familiar ingredients and combine them in a whole new way? That's just what I love doing for you!

$3\frac{1}{2}$ cups cold milk
1 package (4-serving size) instant vanilla pudding and pie filling
1 teaspoon vanilla extract
3 tablespoons any flavor brandy or liqueur (optional)

In a large bowl, combine the milk, pudding mix, and vanilla extract; mix with a wire whisk until well blended. Add the brandy, if desired, and continue whisking until blended thoroughly. Let the sauce stand for 10 minutes, or until slightly thickened. Serve immediately, or chill until ready to use.

NOTE: If you include the brandy or liqueur, then keep this as an adults-only sauce.

Chocolate Maple Syrup

about 1 cup

We all love maple syrup, and we all love chocolate. Never thought of putting them together? Now's the time!

1 cup maple syrup
1/4 cup semisweet chocolate chips

In a small saucepan, combine the syrup and chocolate chips over low heat. Stir constantly until the chocolate chips are completely melted. Serve warm over pancakes, French toast, or waffles.

NOTE: This does the trick to make frozen waffles seem homemade special. And how 'bout trying it over Chocolate Chip Pancakes (page 12)?

Chocolate Frosting

about 2½ cups

For a real chocolate-on-chocolate taste, nothing beats this frosting over a moist chocolate cake!

½ cup (1 stick) butter
¾ cup unsweetened cocoa
½ cup milk
4 cups (1 pound) confectioners' sugar
2 teaspoons vanilla extract

In a small saucepan, melt the butter over medium-low heat. Add the cocoa and stir constantly until smooth. Pour the mixture into a medium-sized bowl and allow to cool. Add the milk and blend with an electric beater on medium speed until smooth. Add the confectioners' sugar 1 cup at a time, blending thoroughly after each addition. Add the vanilla and beat on high speed until smooth and creamy.

NOTE: This makes enough frosting for an 8- or 9-inch layer cake or a 9" × 13" sheet cake.

Buttercream Frosting

about 2 cups

So creamy, so smooth, any cake will seem naked without it!

½ cup (1 stick) butter, softened
4 cups (1 pound) confectioners' sugar
1 teaspoon vanilla extract
¼ cup milk

In a medium-sized bowl, with an electric beater on medium speed, beat the butter until creamy. Add the remaining ingredients and blend until smooth. If not using immediately, cover and chill until ready to use. Bring to room temperature before using.

NOTE: This is a creamy, rich frosting or filling for almost any cake.

Peppermint Frosting

about 2 cups

This has a cool, refreshing mint flavor that makes it a perfect topping for after-dinner goodies.

10 red-and-white peppermint hard candies, unwrapped
½ cup (1 stick) butter, softened
1 teaspoon vanilla extract
¼ cup cold water
4 cups (1 pound) confectioners' sugar

In a blender on high speed or in a food processor that has been fitted with its steel cutting blade, crush the candies into a fine powder. Place the powdered candy in a medium-sized bowl and add the butter and vanilla; mix well. Add the water, blend well, then add the confectioners' sugar 1 cup at a time, blending thoroughly with an electric beater on medium speed after each addition.

NOTE: This makes enough frosting for an 8- or 9-inch layer cake or a 9" × 13" sheet cake. If you'd rather not bring out the blender or food processor, you can make this even easier by substituting 1 teaspoon mint extract for the crushed hard candies. (And you can even add 8 to 10 drops green food color, if you'd like.)

Coffee Frosting

about 3/4 cup

Who could ask for anything better in a frosting? You might not need to make coffee, too, since it's already in here!

1/2 cup heavy cream
1 teaspoon instant coffee granules
1 cup (6 ounces) semisweet chocolate chips
1/2 cup confectioners' sugar

In a small heavy saucepan, combine the cream and coffee over medium heat and stir until the coffee dissolves. Add the chocolate chips and stir until melted and smooth. Remove from the heat and stir in the confectioners' sugar. Chill until the frosting reaches spreading consistency.

NOTE: This makes enough to frost the top of an 8-inch square cake or pan of brownies.

Caramel Frosting

2 cups

Caramel frosting?! Yup! I know we're used to chocolate, vanilla, and buttercream frostings, but why not go for a change this time . . . a surprising, delicious one.

½ cup (1 stick) butter
1 cup firmly packed light brown sugar
¼ cup milk
2 cups (½ pound) confectioners' sugar

In a medium-sized saucepan, melt the butter over medium heat. Add the brown sugar and bring to a boil; cook for 2 minutes, stirring constantly. Add the milk, then return the mixture to a boil. Remove from the heat and allow to cool. Add the confectioners' sugar and stir until smooth.

NOTE: This is perfect for topping your favorite cakes and cupcakes (it'll top about 2 dozen). Why, I've even used it on store-bought pound cakes—my gang thinks I make the whole thing from scratch. I won't tell if you won't!

Chocolate–Cream Cheese Frosting

about 3 cups

White cream cheese frosting looks fabulous over chocolate cake. So, with this frosting on a white cake, we get to turn the tables . . . and it's as good a team as ever!

1 cup (2 sticks) butter, softened
1 package (8 ounces) cream cheese, softened
1 teaspoon vanilla extract
1/4 cup unsweetened cocoa
2 cups (1/2 pound) confectioners' sugar

In a large bowl, with an electric beater on medium speed, beat the butter and cream cheese until creamy. Add the vanilla and cocoa and continue beating until thoroughly mixed. Add the confectioners' sugar gradually, continuing to mix until well blended.

NOTE: For plain Cream Cheese Frosting, just delete the cocoa and add an additional 1/4 cup confectioners' sugar. Since this cream cheese frosting isn't as sweet as other frostings, I like to use this to generously frost an 8- or 9-inch layer cake or a 9" × 13" sheet cake.

Chocolate Glaze

½ cup

I don't know about you, but I think one of the prettiest ways to decorate a cake is to simply drizzle glaze over the top. Boy, this Chocolate Glaze tastes just as good as it looks.

¼ cup sugar
2 teaspoons cornstarch
⅓ cup water
½ ounce (½ square) unsweetened chocolate
½ teaspoon vanilla extract

In a small saucepan, combine the sugar, cornstarch, water, and chocolate over low heat. Cook, stirring constantly, until the chocolate is melted and the mixture is thickened, bubbly, and smooth. Remove from the heat, stir in the vanilla, and use immediately.

Quick Rum Glaze

⅓ cup

Here's an easy way to give ordinary cookies and cakes a fun kick!

¾ cup confectioners' sugar
1 tablespoon light rum
1 tablespoon water

In a small bowl, combine all of the ingredients with a wire whisk until smooth. Drizzle over cool or room-temperature cake or cookies.

NOTE: For a traditional white glaze, you can replace the rum with a tablespoon of water.

Whipped Cream

2 cups

Sure, you can buy the frozen or canned whipped toppings, but for those times when you feel like having fresh, homemade whipped cream, go ahead and whip it yourself. It's so simple and satisfying.

½ pint (1 cup) heavy cream
1 tablespoon sugar

In a medium-sized bowl, with an electric beater on high speed, whip the cream for 1 minute. Add the sugar and continue whipping for 3 to 4 more minutes, or until stiff peaks form.

NOTE: If you're using this to top a sweet dessert, it's probably fine as is. But if you prefer sweet whipped cream, use an additional tablespoon or two of sugar.

Index

Mr. Food Cooks Like Mama

A

THE
MR. FOOD
COOKBOOK
OOH it's so GOOD!!

B

EASY, QUICK, FUN RECIPES
MR. FOOD
COOKS
CHICKEN
"OOH IT'S SO GOOD!!"

C

EASY, QUICK, FUN RECIPES
MR. FOOD
COOKS
PASTA
"OOH IT'S SO GOOD!!"

D

EASY, QUICK, FUN RECIPES
MR. FOOD
MAKES
DESSERT
"OOH IT'S SO GOOD!!"

E

Mr. Food Cooks
R·E·A·L
AMERICAN
EASY, QUICK, FUN RECIPES
"OOH IT'S SO GOOD!!"

F

Mr. Food's
FAVORITE COOKIES
EASY, QUICK, FUN RECIPES
"OOH IT'S SO GOOD!!"

G

Mr. Food's
Quick and Easy Side Dishes

H

Mr. Food
Grills It All in a Snap
OOH IT'S SO GOOD!!

I

Mr. Food®'s Library Gives You More Ways to Say. . . "OOH IT'S SO GOOD!!™"

WILLIAM MORROW

J

K

L

M

N

O